Imagine Buildings
Floating Like Clouds

Vladimir Belogolovsky

Imagine Buildings Floating Like Clouds

Thoughts and Visions on Contemporary
Architecture from 101 Key Creatives

images
Publishing

Contents

"Cherish those who seek the truth but beware of those who find it."

Voltaire

During my November 2016 interview with Eduardo Souto de Moura, at his office in Porto, the Portuguese architect explained, "When I teach, I give all my students one site, one program, one problem, and I want to see 100 solutions, 100 attitudes." That position resonated with me. And when an opportunity to produce this book of interviews for Images Publishing came up, I immediately thought of assembling a collection of 100 contrasting ways that architecture could be imagined (in the process it became 101). I set out to select one essential part—a single question and answer—from 101 of my interviews with architects. Each would expose the complexity of their thinking process, while comparing and contrasting them to one another. I believe these very personal testimonies can help to bring light to many thought-provoking ideas and open up new possibilities.

I've been discussing concepts and schemes with architects regularly for almost 20 years. Since 2002, I have conducted more than 400 one-on-one, multi-hour interviews in New York City and while on business trips to more than 30 countries. As I started compiling my 101-list for this project, I realized that to convey the idea of diversity more fully, in addition to architects, I should also include artists, designers, photographers, and critics who engage with architecture to bring their valuable perspectives and observations into our common discourse. As a result, the book represents key creatives who work in diverse places culturally and climatically and came of age in very different times—from the revolutionary 1960s to our own time, when the future, for many, is being more feared than desired.

Most of the interviews in this book were recorded years ago and were only slightly edited, while some were conducted specifically for this book, during the 2020/2021 coronavirus pandemic, when I started using web-based video conferencing tools for the first time. These long-distance video interviews were quite effective, and I plan to continue using this technology in the future. As I progressed with the project, I kept swapping names into and out of my 101-list to achieve strong contrasts between various views. The final tally includes 72 architects (18 are Pritzker Prize winners), 12 artists, eight photographers, two designers, two historians, two critics, one curator, one urbanist, and one engineer—they are originally from 42 countries and now based in 27. We discussed their intentions, visions, dreams, fears, and hopes. Each Q&A is accompanied by a portrait, and one to three images of my choice.

I practiced architecture for 12 years and I remember searching for my own distinctive direction, my personal voice, and attitude. I had my favorite architects and projects that closely reflected my views. I also recall those who I wholeheartedly opposed. However, as I started meeting with many leading architects to discuss their work, I tried to analyze the diversity of their intentions and sources of inspirations. As I moved from practicing architecture to curating exhibitions and writing books, I learned to respect all architects and their very diverse visions. The point was to be open to different approaches so they could be understood, not merely either embraced or dismissed. I found great pleasure in discovering and documenting these new visions, no matter how quirky and misaligned with my own preferences they might be. Even more satisfaction came from sharing those findings through my publications, lectures, and exhibitions. To me, every conversation is about immersing oneself into a particular narrative. There are stories behind every project and every personality. There is so much more than the architecture in front of you. I learned worlds through these dialogues, and many triggered even deeper inquiries.

Having done so many interviews I began to notice that over the last decade or so, actually starting immediately after the 2012 Venice Architecture Biennale, directed by David Chipperfield under the rubric *Common Ground*, parts of my conversations started to overlap, with similar words and phrases repeated over and over. Extra effort is now required on my part to extract what our leading architects really think. There is now a strong and ongoing tendency to move away from the idea of architect as the sole author of a building. The focus has completely shifted from being egocentric to eco-sensitive, from celebrating artistic originality to seeking collaboration, from crafting an architectural object and dreaming up iconic forms to creating socially engaging environments. There is an increased emphasis on blurring the boundaries between just about everything—programs, building types, even historical times—and identifying and solving problems.

While all these changes should be welcomed—and particularly ecological are in fact existential—we no longer can deny that the way architects talk about their work has become suspiciously similar. The range of ideas currently circulating has been converging and now amounts to just a handful. This follows an explicitly dynamic 15-year period—starting with the opening of Frank Gehry's Guggenheim Bilbao in 1997 and ending with the 2012 Venice Architecture Biennale—when the multiplicity of individual voices was celebrated. Since 2012 (in my view, the apex of the profession's most creative moment in recent years) architecture has entered a much more dogmatic period, meaning there is now a formulaic approach to making a "successful" or "correct" project. There is a list of characteristics that must be checked off: addressing social and pragmatic issues? Check! Environmental features? Check! Green roof and plants in general? Check! Public spaces with seating areas? Check! Use of local and recycled materials. Check! In such a prescribed climate mentioning formal qualities or finding inspirations in art, metaphors, or theory has become quite unpopular, if not taboo.

That's why I feel it is urgent that we be reminded of how diverse our sources of inspirations could be. The truth is that once all the social, technical, economic, environmental, and other pragmatic issues are addressed and solved, often we still haven't gotten even close to producing a piece of architecture, let alone a masterpiece. The most important question still sitting right in front of us is—what makes a building architecture? This question needs to be asked again and again. It's a moving target, and this book gathers many answers but inevitably, also many more questions. The more we advance, the more questions we seem to accumulate!

The book's title *Imagine Buildings Floating Like Clouds* reflects Wolf Prix's very first fantasy project, The Cloud, that imagined a new way of living in the future, when interactive inflatable spaces would be controlled with the user's heartbeat! Or, take another idealistic vision by Moshe Safdie who proposed that everyone should have a garden, also expressed in his very first project, Habitat '67. Will Alsop's plea that the ground should be given to people and gardens, not buildings, is another idealistic dream. Can architecture be non-idealistic? Emilio Ambasz demands that every responsible work of architecture must be 100 percent building and 100 percent landscape. While the aforementioned visions are complementary, many others clash head-to-head, as in the case of Odile Decq and Carme Pigem. If the former designs buildings to accentuate speed, the latter relies on her architecture to slow things down. Shigeru Ban designs his houses to be made out of paper, whereas buildings by Antoine Predock emerge right out of the local geology. Daniel Libeskind believes that every building must have a story, in contrast to his former professor Peter Eisenman, who tries to remove any hint of narrative from his theoretically driven abstract work. Liz Diller and Ric Scofidio admit that solving problems is too easy and boring, while Alejandro Aravena places problem-solving above all else. Thom Mayne is a futurist, whereas Lyndon Neri and Rossana Hu celebrate nostalgia. While Ricardo Bofill argues that cities should be allowed to grow naturally and gradually, urbanist Michael Sorkin insisted on the need for designing new cities from scratch. And if Cesar Pelli warned architects not to jump to making sketches before obtaining sufficient information, Álvaro Siza does just that; he admits earnestly that he can't help it. Whose side are you on, anyway?

In this new book I want to distill 101 different ideas by comparing and contrasting them in order to keep the unsettled discourse going. I typically ask all architects very specific questions, and some questions I ask almost everyone. One of them is this: describe your work or the kind of architecture that you would want to achieve in single words or short phrases? For each of the 101 firms and personalities in this book I selected five such answers—505 in total—making sure none repeat. My hope is to see architecture as diverse as these 505 intentions. And the point is NOT for the reader to identify with just a few or many of them, but to generate his or her own. As Michael Sorkin said in our interview, "Let 1,000 theories bloom!"

Vladimir Belogolovsky
New York, February 2021

"A Drawing Can Be More Powerful than Architecture"

In conversation with
Raimund Abraham, Architect

Outdoor restaurant on the Bowery near Cooper Union in Manhattan, New York, USA, April 5, 2002

B. 1933 in Lienz, Austria;
Lived, practiced, and taught in New York, USA

D. 2010 in Los Angeles, USA

Drawing Another Reality
Power of Imagination
Conquer the Site
Seclusion
Silence

Your visionary projects—Times Square Tower, The House with Curtains, *and* The House without Rooms—*are as well-known as your built works—the Austrian Cultural Forum in New York or the residential block at Friedrichstrasse in Berlin. Does it matter for you if a project gets built? How do you see architecture's purpose?*

The most honest moment in life for me is when I pick up a pencil. When I draw, my drawing does not represent a step toward realization of a project. A drawing is an absolutely autonomous reality that I am trying to anticipate. It is a process of anticipation—of how a line becomes an edge, a plane turns into a wall, and the texture of graphite foresees the texture of what will be ultimately built. I believe architecture does not need to be built. The power of architecture is in its architect's imagination. A drawing can be more powerful than architecture because any building is a compromise. The reality is that all you need is a pencil, a piece of paper, and the desire to make architecture.

Portrait: Raimund Abraham (photo © Brigitte Groihofer)
Left: Raimund Abraham, The Austrian Cultural Forum,
New York, USA, 2002 (photo by David-Plakke © The Austrian
Cultural Forum) Above: Raimund Abraham, *9 Houses Tryptic*,
color pencil, 1975, fragment (digital image © Raimund Abraham)

Left: Raimund Abraham, *The House without Rooms,* project, elevation and plan, color pencil, graphite, and cut-and-pasted printed paper on paper, 34 5/8 x 38 1/8 in (87.9 x 96.8 cm), 1974, Gift of The Howard Gilman Foundation (digital image © The Museum of Modern Art/Licensed by SCALA / Art Resource, NY)

Portrait: Vito Acconci (photo © Vito Acconci Studio) **Above:** Vito Acconci Studio with Steven Holl, Storefront for Art and Architecture, Manhattan, New York, USA, 1982 (photo © Paul Warchol)

"I Wanted to Be in the Middle of Things"

You see architecture as an extension of your career as a poet and performance artist. What were your reasons for switching to architecture?

I wanted to be in the middle of things. And you can never be in the middle of a page or book. You are always in front of the book … I would never have written poetry with boxes and letters if I did. Words and letters were always very literal to me. Letters and lines always take over. I even thought that a single page might be more important than the whole book. I am interested in individual pages. I used to experiment with things like writing a poem where each word is in parentheses. Eventually, I sort of run off the page. Writing pushed me out into the third dimension, even though I didn't think I was interested in architecture at all. Except that my high school was just a few blocks away from where the Guggenheim was being built in the late 1950s and I was so fascinated. It seemed like the world had changed. I have never seen a circular building before. But that didn't lead to architecture until much later, in the 1970s. Maybe I didn't want to face the fact that soon I would be doing something like that. Maybe I was afraid. [Laughs.] Most of all, I don't like any kind of art that only allows you to be in front of it. The idea of being in front of something, but not inside of it, is terrifying to me … And I don't like exhibitions. I like action and interaction. I like things to mean or to be two or three different things. Like in the case of the Storefront we designed with Steven [Holl] the façade turns into hinged walls, windows, seats, platforms … I like motion. I want things to change. Architecture is the opposite of an image. Architecture is about motion and experience. Architecture should not be straightforward. It should be intuitive and multifunctional. I don't like just one person's idea. I like to share and exchange many ideas. And I don't like when everyone agrees. We shouldn't all agree. Otherwise, we would all be the same, wouldn't we?

In conversation with
Vito Acconci, Conceptual Artist

Artist's studio in Brooklyn,
New York, USA, July 30, 2015

B. 1940 in The Bronx, New York,
USA; Lived in New York, USA

D. 2017 in Manhattan,
New York, USA

Multifunctional
Changeable
Portable
Political
Motion

"Looking Is Tough, Most People Project"

In conversation with David Adjaye of Adjaye Associates, Architect

Architect's studio in London, UK, April 23, 2008

B. 1966 in Dar es Salaam, Tanzania; Lives and practices in New York, USA; London, UK; and Accra, Ghana

Rejecting a Cold Perfect Machine

Making and Remaking People's Desires

A New Utopia

No Signature

You worked for Souto de Moura in the beginning of your career. He said: "The building site is whatever you want it to be. The solution never comes from the site, but always from people's heads." How do you view the importance of site?

I think our job, as architects, is to come up with propositions, which are placed out there for the public to identify with certain meanings. If the public can cognitively react in a way that would claim the building into their context, then you succeed in making this local connectivity. It is a way of working with phenomenological and physiological topographies of scales and spaces that recognizes the existing context and identifies the new one. For example, our proposal for a new Skolkovo School of Management on the outskirts of Moscow was about imagining another utopia. The idea of an educational campus is one of the last moments that you can make a utopia because, in a way, a college campus is a perfect monastic place, an idyllic paradise far away from the real world. I thought, we have this idea of a fantastic utopia in Moscow where it snows a great deal. Our competitors proposed traditional college campuses and I proposed a kind of a vertical city on top of a massive disk that connects to the landscape and within that disk there are public squares, plazas and open spaces, residential and leisure facilities. My clients realized that getting from one building to the next in cold winter or hot summer is unpleasant. So, why project the idea of a campus where there is no need for it? That's how the idea of a new utopia occurred. The project came out of a discourse. One of the ways of looking at any site is not to try to fill it up with the image of what your ideal site of that image may be. This strategy forces architects to really look and observe. And looking is tough, most people project.

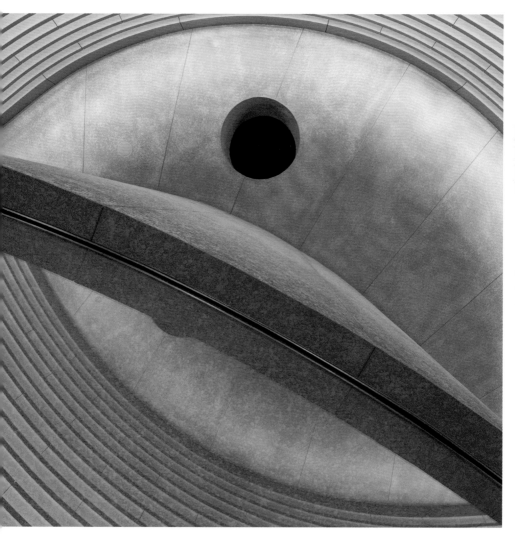

Portrait: David Adjaye (photo © Alex Fradkin) **Above:** Adjaye Associates,
The Webster, Los Angeles, USA, 2020 (photo © Laurian Ghinițoiu)

Opposite: Adjaye Associates, Moscow School of Management Skolkovo, Moscow, Russia, 2010 (photo © Denis Esakov, 2010)
Above: Adjaye Associates, Moscow School of Management Skolkovo, Moscow, Russia, 2010 (photo © Ilya Ivanov, 2016)

Portrait: Will Alsop (photo © Will Alsop and All Design, London) Top: Will Alsop and All Design, The Sharp Centre, Ontario College of Art and Design, Toronto, Canada, 2004 (photo © Richard Johnson) Bottom left: Will Alsop and All Design, The Sharp Centre, Ontario College of Art and Design, Toronto, Canada, 2004 (photo © Tom Arban) Bottom right: A painting by Will Alsop from the architect's Toronto series paintings, 2006 (painting © Will Alsop and All Design, London)

"The Ground Should Be Given to People and Gardens, Not Buildings"

What is a good honest building for you, and how do you try to achieve it?

When it has a good quality of construction, good lighting, and particularly—paying attention to what is happening at the bottom because that is what most people experience. If I were a politician, I would make a law in every city that everything from the ground to 10 meters and higher should float and not touch the ground. You could still eat and drink at the ground level, but there would be no buildings. The ground should be given to people and gardens, not buildings. It would make our cities much happier. More importantly, architecture is not about just having a roof over your head, but about a feeling of belonging and feeling comfortable. Sometimes it is very difficult to explain how to do that, but I had people who told me that my buildings are very comfortable. They would come to me and ask, "How do you do that?" I don't know and I don't want to know because if I did all the fun and exploration about making architecture would be destroyed. You have to have fate ... We are all settled with our cultural baggage. But I think our job is to go beyond that and to see what the possibilities are out there. I am interested in how buildings affect communities ... How do I achieve a good building? I do very different things and in different ways. Some people say—there is an Alsop style. It is an insult to me because I like to avoid it. I have gone away from the idea of what architecture should be. My job is to discover what architecture could be. There is no right way to make architecture and I think that is good. Our cities should have diversity. Uniformity makes life less interesting ... One of the reasons I like painting is that you are not really in control of what you are doing, and that interests me a lot. I see the art of architecture in putting everything together in your own way.

In conversation with
Will Alsop, Architect

Architect's studio in London, UK,
October 22, 2010

B. 1947 in Northampton, UK;
Lived in London, UK
D. 2018 in London, UK

Exchange of Ideas
Aspirations
Diversity
Beauty
Fun

"I Detest Writing Theories, I Prefer Writing Fables"

In conversation with Emilio Ambasz, Architect and Designer

Architect's home in Bologna, Italy, July 12, 2015

B. 1943 in Resistencia, Chaco, Argentina; Lives in Bologna, Italy

100 Percent Building and 100 Percent Landscape
An Act of the Myth-Making Imagination
Emotions
Intuition
Ritual

I look at your oeuvre as an archetypal quest to reimagine such ritualistic and processional projects as primitive huts, caves, ancient astronomical observatories, terraced gardens, ziggurats, labyrinths, amphitheaters, tomb ruins, and so on. Is there one particular project that you still would like to do? What ideas would you like to explore?

I don't know until they come to me. I am not an intellectual. I detest writing theories. I prefer writing fables. They are metaphors. That's what metaphors are philosophically. A metaphor is a model for approximation. I don't work with words. When I design, I try to remove all words from my mind, and I work with images. Because if I work with words I will remain in the semantic domain, which is something already understood. But I am interested in images that come to me without being conscious about them until they simply come. And I am not aware of their meanings until I start thinking. Then I start asking questions. This was the case with my Casa de Retiro Espiritual. I could come up with a whole theory about that project, but it came to me as a complete image. I think it is a great tragedy when the word arrives before the image …

My work is a search for giving architectural form to primal things—being born, being in love, and dying. I strive with my architecture to show one way to reconcile architecture with nature. I always try that my buildings return to the community in the form of gardens, as much as the building's footprint covers. I believe, the task of an architect is always the same: to give poetic form to the pragmatic.

Portrait: Emilio Ambasz (photo © G. Porcarelli) **Above:** Emilio Ambasz, Casa de Retiro Espiritual, Seville, Spain, 2004 (photo © Michele Alassio)

Portrait: Refik Anadol (photo © Serge Hoeltschi) **Above:** Refik Anadol Studio, *Machine Hallucination*, New York, USA, 2019–20 (photo by Refik Anadol, courtesy Refik Anadol Studio)

"What Will Happen If Machines Start Dreaming?"

You convert data into parametric data sculptures and paintings. You call this process data visualization and data dramatization. You also refer to such visualizations as dreams of a machine. How is it possible for a machine to dream?

This, of course, is a speculation. We know that machines can't dream yet. But we also know that machines can learn very quickly from the patterns of our own cognitive systems and, potentially, even generate their own ideas. So, I am very optimistic that eventually, machines will start hallucinating and dreaming. What I am trying to show is a glimpse of an idea, a glimpse of the future. What will happen if machines start dreaming? What I like to explore is not to imagine humans becoming like machines, but making machines becoming more like humans. We will continue to learn from each other, and we'll evolve together ... My work is a journey [as we speak, Anadol is driving his car along Santa Monica Freeway from his office in Central LA to the UCLA where he has been teaching mediated space, media arts, and motion]. Every time I explain what I do a little differently because I am on a journey, and I don't entirely know where exactly I am heading. But fundamentals don't change. What's changing constantly is technology—data, algorithms, and space ... I believe architecture can go beyond its functions; it will learn to have a dialogue with us, to respond to our needs. It will be able to live with us even on an emotional level and, again, it will be able to dream with us ... Everything we know can one day be seen, heard, felt, touched, and all at once. The world we know today— architecture of concrete, steel, and glass—is just three dimensions. The machines will help us to transform the idea of space into something much more sensual. That world will change architecture in more ways that we can possibly predict today ... My key intention is how to give depth to a surface. Architecture will become more humanistic and, in a way, humanized. Imagine, what could happen if we teach a building to dream! Can we control the way we dream? What is the meaning or purpose of dreams? How do dreams make an effect on us? How can we learn from our dreams?

In conversation with
Refik Anadol, Media Artist

Skype video call between
New York and Los Angeles, USA,
February 6, 2020

B. 1985 in Istanbul, Turkey;
Lives in Los Angeles, USA

Hallucinations and
Dreams
Curiosity and
Speculation
A Glimpse of the Future
What Is Real?
Digital Space

"Solutions Have to Be Invented, Not Solved"

In conversation with
Paul Andreu, Architect

Architect's studio in Paris,
France, November 15, 2016

B. 1938 in Caudéran, France;
Lived and practiced in Paris,
France

D. 2018 in Paris, France

Organic System
Pure Breathing
Human Place
Being Bold
Dreaming

You have designed at least 60 airport terminals, 25 of which were built all over the world. Do you think there is a benefit of specializing in a particular building type?

Yes and no. The best architecture happens when you can reinvent a concept and not just work on packaging things. When I started, it was a great time for airports. Back then you could do that, we constantly experimented with new ideas, as airports were growing and changing all the time. Everything was so new. There was no past. The very first commercial airports started to appear in the 1920s. So, by 2000, working on airports for almost 40 years, I was involved in designing this building type for half of its existence, and it really started to grow and change dramatically right at the time when I started. Airports no longer change; they just grow in size; there is no new concept. And, unfortunately, now many seemingly different building types converge around the shopping experience. There are airport versions of commercial malls, railway station versions, or museum versions. Everything is a commercial center. Anyway, I no longer work on airports. After a major accident in May 2004, when a portion of the roof collapsed at the Terminal 2E at Charles de Gaulle Airport, killing four people. It was such a huge shock. I was not charged with any wrongdoing, as it was a structural failure, but my major project at the time, a large casino and hotel complex in Macao was put on hold and I had to let go my entire staff, dozens of people. At that moment, I thought I would quit architecture completely, but I decided to stay. I shifted to other sectors ... To achieve something interesting you have to ask questions and not just solve problems. Solutions have to be invented, not solved. And there is nothing wrong with a process, in which every line is a doubt. You search for your conviction. Once you have it, it is all about following through and convincing everyone else.

Portrait: Paul Andreu (photo courtesy Paul Andreu) **Above:** Paul Andreu, Terminal 1,
Charles de Gaulle Airport, Paris, France, 1967–74 (photo © Paul Maurer)

Portrait: Alejandro Aravena (photo © Victor Oddo) Above: Alejandro Aravena, Elemental, Santa Catarina, Nuevo Leon, Mexico, 2008–10 (photo © Ramiro Ramírez)

"My Way to Improve the Reality Is by Building"

Wolf Prix told me that his students "learn to shape their ideas not conditioned by the reality of constraints and clichés, but by the reality of possibilities." In other words, students imagine what is possible. And isn't it true that the most imaginative projects get built not only because we need them, but because there are clients and architects who can imagine them? Do you agree?

No, I don't. You need to know exactly what the goal is. If you give me some objects and say—produce fire with them, I can come up with many solutions, but all of them will fail if, at the end of the day, there is no fire. If you just give me these objects and I have all the freedom in the world to do anything I want, then it is meaningless. There is no tension, no purpose, no way of measuring whether I have succeeded or not. I believe creativity comes from overcoming the constraints. For example, agriculture was not invented just by playing with possibilities. And there would be no fire if people were not dying of hunger ... Here in Chile, we are faced with very concrete problems and that's why I am very critical of arbitrary gestures in architecture. I am doing architecture for a reason. I want to build projects better than they were done before, not just different. And better, not just as far as design, but better in terms of the living conditions ... You see, in academia people often invent problems to be solved. But we live in a world, which already has so many problems. Why should I introduce another set of problems into the world already full of them? For example, wouldn't it be good to be able to change lives of poor people living in our cities? Elemental is a "do tank" not just think tank. If I want to change something in my city, I don't write a letter to the newspaper, I do something. My way to improve the reality is by building. Fifteen years ago, I had an idea for 14-kilometer uninterrupted pedestrian park, Santiago Metropolitan Promenade. So, I went to see the Mayor and, eventually, the President to push for it. Both positions are now run by their successors and many debates later we now have this project, finally, close to completion. I like to keep a balance between being ambitious and realistic at the same time. I am a dreamer, but with both feet on the ground.

In conversation with
Alejandro Aravena of Elemental,
Architect

Architect's studio in Santiago,
Chile, April 4, 2014

B. 1967 in Santiago, Chile;
Lives in Santiago, Chile

Constraints and
Restrictions
Focus on the Essential
Against Arbitrariness
Synthesis
Dignity

"Our Expertise Is in the Realm of Creating Spatiality"

In conversation with Hani Rashid and Lise Anne Couture of Asymptote Architecture, Architects

Asymptote studio in Long Island City, New York, USA, August 28, 2015

Hani Rashid: B. 1958 in Cairo, Egypt; Lives and practices in New York, USA

Lise Anne Couture: B. 1959 in Montreal, Canada; Lives and practices in New York, USA

Seamless and Timeless
Baroque-like Infinity
Open Flow Elegance
Plasticity of Space
Aligned Precision

I heard phrases from you such as "impeccable spatiality" and "asymptotic trajectory." What animals are these?

HR: Well, our real focus is centered on exploring new spatial possibilities in architecture. We are often described as architects seemingly preoccupied with form and its manipulation with computers and software. However, beneath that "superficial" reading of what preoccupies us is our primary concern that has always been the problem of spatiality itself. In every one of our projects, we attempt to define and explore very precisely, what we might call an "impeccable spatiality." For us such spatiality is central. So, our key focus is centered on exploring new spatial possibilities in architecture. The use of parametric tools and computing in general, gave us the ability to liquify space. For example, the genesis of our Yas Viceroy Hotel was being shrouded in a mercury-like liquid veil. The building is the setting for the Formula 1 races each year; it celebrates speed and fluidity.

LAC: Our expertise is in the realm of creating spatiality; we are spatial engineers rather than architects. We often ask this question—what would you do spatially, formally, and tectonically if there were no physical constraints? And about asymptotic trajectory; that's how we think about our practice. Mathematically, an asymptote describes a curve that approaches a straight line but never meets it. There is something of an analogy here as to how art and architecture relate to each with the stark difference that architecture is really about problem-solving. However, in reality and ironically, I don't think that architects solve problems as much as we resolve solutions. Sure, we are interested in resolving issues, but they can be elusive at best, and as you get closer to a solution, you then discover something else, as a provocation and new problems arise.

Portrait: Lise Anne Couture and Hani Rashid of Asymptote Architecture (photo © Naho Kubota Photography) **Above:** Asymptote Architecture, Yas Viceroy Hotel (now W Abu Dhabi—Yas Island), Abu Dhabi, UAE, 2010 (photo courtesy Asymptote Architecture)

Portrait: Iwan Baan (photo © Jonas Eriksson) **Above:** HHF architects, Baby Dragon Pavilion, Jinhua Architecture Park, Jinhua, Zhejiang Province, China, 2006 (photo © Iwan Baan) **Following pages:** Herzog & de Meuron, National Olympic Stadium, Beijing, China, 2008 (photo © Iwan Baan)

"You Can't Plan a Good Picture, But You Must Be Ready to Take It"

I have a feeling you get more pleasure out of documenting projects than other photographers, as I understand you don't like when architects tell you how to do your work, right?

I tell stories with my images. And there is always a discovery in the process. Learning something new is what I like most. Many architects like to control every aspect of their designs. They can't let it go and they like to control how their buildings are used and represented in the media. Architects don't like things that are beyond their control. [Laughs.] But I don't rehearse anything. No one tells me what to do and how to do it. Luckily, the clients who I choose to work with respect my vision and my personal approach. I am not serving anyone. My clients tell me the name, location, and we look at my work when I get back. In that sense, I want to believe that I am an artist. I am very independent. For me the most interesting part starts when the architect has left, and people start to take over and explore the place how they see fit. I like to capture these moments. And there is no golden hour for me. Places and buildings can look fantastic in very different moments. Pouring rain can be just as perfect as a sunny day. Of course, architects know every detail better than anyone else and they try not to leave much space for any surprise. Yet, so much of photography is all about something unplanned and unexpected. You can't plan a good picture, but you must be ready to take it. I have a real urge to see how people live and I like to tell stories about that. To me these stories are so much bigger than just buildings, particularly when I come across vernacular buildings that people built with their own hands with lots of care. There is an incredible beauty in these things, which is being lost very quickly. So, I have a sense of urgency, a mission of a sort, to document these unique places as much as possible.

In conversation with
Iwan Baan, Photographer

Phone call between New York and Arizona, USA, February 26, 2019

B. 1975 in Alkmaar, The Netherlands;
Lives in Amsterdam,
The Netherlands;
works around the world

Constructing a Narrative
Cities and Public Spaces
Constantly on the Move
Disappearing Cultures
Capturing Life

"I Want to Create My Own Artificiality"

In conversation with Cecil Balmond, Structural Engineer, Architect, Designer, and Artist

Microsoft Teams video call between New York, USA and London, UK, March 24, 2021

B. 1943 in Colombo, Sri Lanka; Lives and practices in London, UK and Colombo, Sri Lanka

Both Objective and Subjective

Bespoke and Improvisation

Self-Organizing Systems

Why Not Skip a Bit?

Nonlinear

You said, "What I am always searching for is a poetic in space." Could you touch on that?

That's true. What is also true is that our profession—both architecturally and in terms of engineering—has retreated from the notion of poetry. It is much more concerned with function, but also spectacular in its extreme manifestation. For me my projects are about achieving a poetic quality, which has to do with tension, balance, and visceral feeling. There is a rhythm, and then there is a break with that rhythm. I use, at times, ideas from biology and cosmology in terms of sequence, overlap, etc. Poetry is about a delirium-like state of being, about reducing a meaning of something to the absolute essence. Most importantly, I never see limitations.

I began my aesthetic search humbly, first by noticing what a piece of structure could do to a space, and I kept pushing my interests from there. I started to see structure as an episodic notion, not a distributed system, not a skeleton. Questioning is important; it opens doors to new discoveries. Anything that's not standardized, modular, and preconceived has a potential to be poetic. Ultimately, the question is this—is it possible to make something that appears irrational into something rational? Here is the root of my interest—whether something is objective or subjective. I have an open mind; I switch from one to the other. We have unbound freedom of doing many things in many ways. I never reduce structure to mere calculation; pattern must be intrinsic to a form. I see it as an organizing power. The root of a solution is in the overlap of science and art, instincts and pragmatism. I am trying to break the formality of any order, modularity, and regularity. I see architecture as a process of building our artificial world, something completely different from nature. I want to create my own artificiality. Certain critics say that my book *informal* was like a brick thrown at the establishment. The truth is that I have no intention attacking anything. I simply want to discover something new.

Portrait: Cecil Balmond (photo by Edward Hull © Balmond Studio) **Above:** Toyo Ito with Cecil Balmond, Serpentine Pavilion 2002, London, UK, appropriated as part of a restaurant in the south of France (photo courtesy Balmond Studio)

Portrait: Shigeru Ban (photo courtesy Shigeru Ban Architects) **Above:** Shigeru Ban Architects, Japanese Pavilion at the World Expo 2000, Hanover, Germany, dismantled (photo © Hiroyuki Hirai)

"How Long Can a Paper House Last?"

Are you the first architect to employ paper as a building material? Aren't paper houses afraid of rain, fire, and cold weather, and can last only temporarily?

A great American engineer, Buckminster Fuller, used paper tubes in his famous geodesic domes. But no one before me built permanent structures primarily out of paper. Of course, when I refer to my paper structures as permanent, what I mean is that no building is really permanent, even if it is built out of stone and steel. Even a concrete building built for profit will not last indefinitely. So, what is permanent and what is temporary, and how long can a paper house last? Forever! It has nothing to do with the material. The worn-out elements can be replaced but the life of a house can potentially go on for as long as there is love and need for it. The same happens with any other building.

Any building, regardless of what it is made of, has to be fireproof and isolated from bad weather. So, what difference does it make what a building is made of? The paper that I use for construction is specially treated to make it fireproof and waterproof. Don't forget that the same cardboard tubes are used to pour wet concrete to make monolithic cylindrical columns. So, this material is well tested. No one argues that wood is stronger than paper and that steel is stronger than wood. But in different situations we prefer one material over another. When I design my buildings, I think not only about how to build them but also how to demolish them later. My Japanese Pavilion at the World Expo 2000 in Hanover was assembled out of materials that could be reused and recycled. After the Expo it was quickly dismantled to avoid creating industrial waste.

In conversation with
Shigeru Ban, Architect

Architect's office in New York,
USA, February 26, 2003

B. 1957 in Tokyo, Japan; Lives and
practices in Tokyo, Japan

Temporary Versus
Permanent
Buildings out of Paper
Working for People
Recycled Materials
Architectonic

"The Goal Is to Create an Immortal Building"

In conversation with
Boris Bernaskoni, Architect

Author's apartment in
Long Island City, New York, USA,
February 1, 2019

B. 1977 in Moscow, Russia;
Lives and practices in
Moscow, Russia

Beauty Is in the
Engineering
Algorithmic
Architecture
Hyper-functionality
AI and Big Data
Interface

You don't think that the idea of an architect as an artist is still relevant?

That's the architect's role—to manifest oneself, as an artist, to cut everything extraneous, like Michelangelo, and leave everything that's essential to the place, function, and the time that we live in. A good architect must be able to achieve that at the highest technical and artistic level. A building is not just a sculpture, but also a structure that must function well and be profitable. The goal is to create an immortal building, a kind of building that would be able to transform from a caterpillar into a butterfly, retaining its essence but metamorphosing into something entirely new over time, depending on the future challenges. The ability of a building to be able to transform into something new is one of the most vital functions of architecture in the future. I would compare a modern building to a computer's motherboard with chips responsible for numerous functions. This is how I see my architecture. Transformation, hybridization, and hyper-functionality are the three notions that I always explore in my architecture. However, architecture begins when a building sets on a mission. Architecture's biggest commodity is its ability to transform. It is the transformation that enables buildings to be immortal and remain relevant.

Portrait: Boris Bernaskoni (photo
by Eric Panov © BERNASKONI)
Above: BERNASKONI, Villa Mirror
Mongayt, Near Moscow, Russia,
2010 (photo © Vladislav Efimov)
Left: BERNASKONI, Hypercube at
Skolkovo Innovation Center, Moscow,
Russia, 2012 (photo © Yuri Palmin)

Portrait: Aaron Betsky (photo © Andrew Pielage) **Above:** Cesar Pelli, Pacific Design Center, West Hollywood, Los Angeles, USA, 1975–2012 (photo © Pelli Clarke Pelli Architects)

"We Live in a Culture of Effects"

In conversation with
Aaron Betsky, Curator and Critic

You said, "Architecture is the styling of buildings into something seductive." Don't you think that this notion is very superficial?

Hey, you are a real fundamentalist, aren't you? [Laughs.] Well, yes, it is superficial because it is about surfaces, absolutely. Cesar Pelli once said: "Architecture is a question of a quarter of an inch." Especially in places like New York architecture is often just a skin job. Let's face it—buildings are defined more and more by codes. By financial codes, linguistic codes, safety codes, building codes, codes of behavior, and so on. So, what the architect has left to play with is the skin and a few public spaces. If that is the space, you have, then do something with it. We live in a culture of effects, meaning that how things are produced is invisible. Everything is coming out of a little box. So, what you have are continuously changing effects and if architecture has to operate in that kind of culture then it has to operate on the level of effects. There are various strategies of resistance or avoidance, but I think it is important for architects to organize a chaos of effects into something apprehensive and revealing.

I also think that the notion that architecture should be built for the ages is highly overrated. What interests me is the architecture that remains unfinished, that has the quality of leaving enough bits and pieces that are unsaid or unrealized but points toward its potential for completion or elaboration.

Starbucks Café near Museum
of Modern Art, Manhattan,
New York, USA, March 28, 2005

B. 1958 in Missoula, Montana,
USA; Lives and teaches in
Charlottesville, Virginia, USA

A Belief in a Better World
Beyond Buildings
Nonstatic Space
No Fixed Ground
Repurposing

"Architecture Should Benefit Every Single Human Being on This Planet"

In conversation with
Tatiana Bilbao, Architect

Architect's studio in Mexico City, Mexico, June 16, 2017

B. 1972 in Mexico City, Mexico; Lives in Mexico City, Mexico and teaches in the USA

Architecture Needs to Be Provoking

Platform for a Conversation

Building a Community

Utopia Has Died

People First

The more I talk to architects, the more it becomes apparent that architecture has no boundaries. It is not just about buildings, but rather about building communities. Yet, it wasn't this way as recently as when we were students, in the 1990s, right?

You are right. Architecture is not about building a building; architecture is about building a community. We started our firm with Fernando Romero and other partners in 1998, right after my graduation. It was an important moment here in Mexico. The economy suddenly took off. In the 1980s and 1990s there was one financial crisis after another, it was impossible for architecture to emerge. Back then, at the time of the generation of Alberto Kalach and Enrique Norten, it was hard to survive. But by the time our generation was out of school the economy stabilized and Mexico emerged as a global player. Architecture became a trend globally, especially following Guggenheim Bilbao by Frank Gehry. My generation capitalized on these changes. We were active and wanted to be independent. We didn't know how we were going to do our architecture, but we wanted to be a part of the global scene and to be open to all kinds of happenings in architecture, art, and culture. We organized exhibitions, invited important curators and architects to share their ideas; we designed utopian houses for artists. We explored so many possibilities. And we did what everyone was doing—the blobs. We were preoccupied by the forms we could do and how we could amaze the world with them.

Then, in 2004, I realized that I wanted to do something completely different from my partners. I started my independent practice with one fundamental idea— architecture should benefit every single human being on this planet. The benefit can't be abstract; it has to be about the individual. Architecture must have an impact on a broad level and that's why it needs to be conceived by many different people, not just the architects.

Portrait: Tatiana Bilbao (photo by Ana Hop © Tatiana Bilbao ESTUDIO) **Above:** Tatiana Bilbao ESTUDIO, Ways of Life, Waldeck, Germany, conceptual drawing, 2017 (drawing courtesy Tatiana Bilbao ESTUDIO)

Portrait: Stefano Boeri (photo by Giovanni Gastel © Boeri Studio)
Above: Boeri Studio, Bosco Verticale (Vertical Forest), Milan, Italy, 2014 (drone shot of green façade by Paolo Aralla © Boeri Studio)

48

"Observing the World Through the Filter of the Leaves and Branches"

I like your description of Bosco Verticale, "A house for trees and birds, inhabited also by humans." That flips the argument—you don't view these trees as mere décor, the house is really for them. And could you touch on specific inspirations behind this project?

Absolutely, the idea was to build a tower for trees—which, incidentally, housed human beings. As far as the most immediate inspiration, that came from Italo Calvino, and particularly, his novel, *The Baron in the Trees*, in which a young baron abandons his noble family, climbs the trees and vows never to set foot on the earth again. It is in the trees that he starts making friends, he then falls in love, and so on. The entire novel is about a life in the trees. It is a fantasy, of course. What I like about it is that what is plausible can become possible—this idea of observing the world through the filter of the leaves and branches. That's the image I had while working on Bosco Verticale. That has become real—people who live there see the world through the filter of these amazing leaves and branches.

Then there are such precedents as buildings by Emilio Ambasz, and another person was Friedensreich Hundertwasser, an Austrian architect. His Hundertwasserhaus apartment block in Vienna has large trees growing from inside the apartments, as their branches are coming out of the windows. I have a strong memory of seeing him in the streets of Milan—walking with a tree when he came here in 1972 on the invitation of the Triennale di Milano. His message was very important—he insisted on treating trees as tenants or inhabitants. He treated the tree as a partner of man and advocated for the rights of nature to be reinstated, as they were taken away by man illegally. These people, as well as a popular song by Adriano Celentano, "Un Albero Di Trenta Piani (A 30-Story Tree)" had opened the imagination to the new kind of architecture.

In conversation with
Stefano Boeri, Architect

Architect's office in Milan, Italy,
May 27, 2021

B. 1956 in Milan, Italy; Lives and
practices in Milan, Italy

Unique Visions of a
Room and a City
Connecting People
and Nature
Limit Urban Expansion
Life in the Trees
Civic Relevance

"Why Are Historical Towns More Beautiful than Modern Cities?"

In conversation with
Ricardo Bofill, Architect

Architect's studio in Barcelona,
Spain, February 25, 2016

B. 1939 in Barcelona, Spain;
Lives and practices in
Barcelona, Spain

Critical, Personal,
and Unsatisfied

Reinterpreting
Modern City

Traditional Towns

Work in Progress

Genius Loci

In the early 1980s, your new social housing towns on the outskirts of Paris and the Antigone development in Montpellier in the South of France assumed an illusion of luxurious palaces and modern reinterpretation of French gardens. Could you touch on the origins of those designs at the time, which was the highpoint of postmodernism?

While working on those projects in France, I was addressing a simple issue—why are historical towns more beautiful than modern cities? I was trying to prove that the opposite was possible. I experimented with prefabrication techniques and ways of providing so much social housing for so many migrants coming to France at the time. You need to rely on a lot of repetition in construction to build new cities economically. The classical period also had a lot of repetition with each part being very beautiful. So, what we were doing then was reinterpreting and reinventing the vocabulary of a modern city where we referenced history and relied on the latest technology. Classical architecture became for me a fountain of inspiration. The idea was to recover some of the historical elements of architecture, the tradition that was cut off in the 1920s and 1930s when architecture became *tabula rasa,* as the Fathers of modernism had a total disregard for history.

But when postmodernism became accepted and popular after the 1980 Venice Biennale, it turned into a style and quickly became ironic, even vulgar. Once it became a movement, I was no longer interested. It is important to have an engine inside of you to provoke change and evolution, to be unsatisfied and critical of your own work, and to keep this internal engine constantly running. Back then I was trying to combine the best of modernism and the best of classicism. I still like classical architecture, its notions of sequence of spaces, system of proportions, and the strive for perfection. But today I try to avoid following any style. Instead, we incorporate new technology, ecology, and our own history to write architecture like a novelist would write a book.

Portrait: Ricardo Bofill (photo by Nacho Alegre © Taller de Arquitectura [RBTA]) Above: Taller de Arquitectura (RBTA), La Muralla Roja, Calpe, Alicante, Spain, 1973 (photo © Gregori Civera) Left: *Les Arcades du Lac*, Paris, France, 1982 (drawing by Ricardo Bofill © Taller de Arquitectura [RBTA])

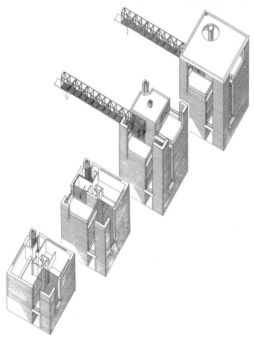

Portrait: Mario Botta (photo © Nicola Gnesi)
Above: Mario Botta Architetti, Casa Bianchi,
Riva San Vitale, Switzerland, 1971–73
(photo © Alo Zanetta) Left: Mario Botta
Architetti, Casa Bianchi, Riva San Vitale,
Switzerland, 1971–73 (axonometric
projection by Mario Botta, courtesy Mario
Botta Architetti) Following pages: Mario Botta
Architetti, Church San Giovanni Battista, Mongo,
Switzerland, 1986–96 (photo © Enrico Cano)

"I Work in the Territory of Memory"

You said, "You don't need a Moon-landing technology to make a house." It is true, your houses are being built today the same way they were built in the past. Could you touch on your architecture's reliance on history?

Nowadays, there is a lot of talk about technology—new materials and new building techniques. But for the most part, I don't see why houses and some other projects can't be built more or less the way they were built for centuries. Even if modern technology allows us to reach the Moon, why can't we live in a very simple house without a lot of sophistication? I am trying to achieve a sense of timelessness, not to bring all the latest sophistication. Our body is the same as in the past, our needs are basically the same as before. I think contemporary architecture often overexaggerates the importance of technology, both as far as buildings' forms and non-traditional cladding materials. But if you ever lived in traditional houses in Venice or Florence—with thick walls, high ceilings, and small windows, you would agree that these places offer very high standards of living and the quality of life there can be very satisfactory. You ask me whether the latest technology should be a part of architecture. But, as an architect, I work in the territory of memory. Today, we often forget the past, but I am inspired by the past more than by anything else. Today, critics talk about technology, sociology, ecology, biology … But they forget about perhaps the most important reference, and that is our own history. What I do is not invented from scratch. My work is rooted in both history of the discipline and history of each place.

In conversation with
Mario Botta, Architect

Architect's studio in Mendrisio,
Switzerland, May 25, 2021

B. 1943 in Mendrisio, Switzerland;
Lives and practices in Mendrisio,
Switzerland

Architecture Starts
with Gravity
I Use Geometry
Without Fear
Presence of Materials
Resisting Banalities
Rooted in History

"My Work Always Starts with Either Being For or Against the Architecture of the Place"

In conversation with
Daniel Buren, Conceptual Artist

Bortolami Gallery in Manhattan,
New York, USA, May 12, 2017

B. 1938 in Boulogne-Billancourt,
France; Lives in Paris, France

Objecting to Traditions
Light and Volume
New Situations
Site-Specific
Obstinacy

What makes your installations different from traditional paintings and how do they relate to architecture?

First, my works are not installations. I call them "works in situ," meaning you cannot take them out and place somewhere else. They can be temporary or permanent, but most importantly, they are intrinsic to the space. Installations are things you see in the vitrines of department stores. You can put them anywhere. I always work with a particular situation and place because, as a visual artist, before you can do anything, you are confronted with architecture. When I realized that, I quit being a painter. Either consciously or subconsciously, first, we are dealing with architecture and people. Before I do anything, I always consider these two key elements. My work is critical; it always starts with either being for or against the architecture of the place. It is the architecture of the place that feeds me with ideas for my work. It is architecture that makes me nervous, confused, or excited. My proposal is never definitive; it is just one of many possibilities, just one solution out of numerous others that could have been just as good.

Traditional paintings are done to blind you! When you try to see the painting, you cannot see the wall. My interest was in making it possible to see the wall or billboard, or curtain, or whatever material I was using. And not only did it become possible to see the wall itself, but also around it and behind; the wall or the background became part of the painting, whereas traditional paintings always were separated from the wall by their frames. For a painting to exist, it must show itself. It can't be neutral. My stripes are completely banal and neutral, so they focus attention to the wall and space. My work is never autonomous. It is a rare idea, don't you think? Maybe I am the only artist who insists on this condition because all the art that was produced from the beginning of time is declared to be autonomous. But I take the liberty and risk to claim that my work is not autonomous. My work is a part of everything around it and it has the power to transform everything around it.

Portrait: Daniel Buren (photo by Claude Truong-Ngoc © Daniel Buren) **Above:** Daniel Buren, *Les Deux Plateaux, cour d'honneur du Palais-Royal*, Paris, France, 1986 (photo © Daniel Buren; courtesy Bortolami Gallery)

Portrait: Alberto Campo Baeza (photo © Alberto Campo Baeza) Top: Alberto Campo Baeza, House of the Infinite, Cádiz, Spain, 2014 (photo © Javier Callejas) Bottom: Alberto Campo Baeza, Andalucia's Museum of Memory, Granada, Spain, 2010 (photo © Javier Callejas)

"Utopia Is Not Impossible"

What are some of the guiding principles behind your work?

Architecture should not be capricious; every project should be like a diagnosis for a particular site and program. There is science behind every project. Design is based on reason. You have to look for an idea capable to be built. Beauty is not a utopian idea. Utopia is not impossible. With new technology utopia can be built. Beauty can be achieved with logic, rationality, harmonious proportions, and appropriate scale. You have to try to be serious, deep, and sincere.

I would rather try to be universal than personal. Gaudí was a genius, but too personal for my taste. When architecture is too unique, it loses a sense of universality. In my work, I try to be simple, quiet, abstract; in short, universal. Sure, this is just the starting point, just the foundation. To achieve real beauty you need imagination, you need inspiration. I focus on such themes as transparency and continuity. Mies did not need to rely on traditional enfilade because he used technology to achieve transparency and continuity. Konstantin Melnikov strived for his architecture to be bare, "To take off her marble dress, remove her make-up and reveal herself as she is, naked, like a young and graceful goddess." Architecture should be serious, which is not the same as boring. It should be consequential; it should be beautiful. Plato said, "Beauty is the splendor of the truth." In other words, beauty is the reflection of reason, not a mere intuitive gesture.

In conversation with
Alberto Campo Baeza, Architect

Architect's studio in Madrid,
Spain, December 2 and 3, 2019

B. 1946 in Valladolid, Spain;
Lives, practices, and teaches
in Madrid, Spain

Restraint Is a
Prerequisite of
Happiness
Suspension of Time
Hymn to Freedom
Order and Clarity
Essentiality

"Why Can't My Forms Come Out of Nature?"

In conversation with
Douglas Cardinal, Architect

Phone call between New York,
USA and Ottawa, Ontario, Canada,
April 24, 2020

B. 1934 in Calgary, Canada;
Lives and practices in Ottawa,
Ontario, Canada

Nurturing, Comforting,
and Protecting
We Are a Part of Nature
Organic Architecture
Spatial Inventions
Commitment

When you were studying architecture in the early 1950s you had trouble with your professors at the University of British Columbia in Vancouver because you felt that boxy buildings were squeezing art out of architecture. What inspired you to pursue your own vision?

I thought those buildings were completely dismissive of the environment and isolated from nature. But I was always convinced that nature is a special gift and must be protected. Nature is beautiful and should be an inspiration to architects. Architecture should be an integral part of nature. Here in Canada in the 1920s and 1930s there was a collective of landscape painters called the Group of Seven. They expressed beautiful forms of nature and were inspired by Canadian landscape. They believed that a distinct Canadian art could be developed through direct contact with nature. I met one of them—Lawren Harris. His abstracted representation of nature was very powerful. When I saw his paintings, I remember saying, "Why can't my forms come out of nature?" And, of course, many works—from Egyptian temples and classical temples to Gothic cathedrals and art nouveau—came out of nature. So, I thought, "Why play with abstract geometric forms made of cold concrete and totally devoid of feelings and relation to the land?!" They were so stark and imposing. I felt that my buildings should grow out of nature and be in harmony with nature and human beings. Many of my structures are either male or female buildings, and some are composed of combinations of both. The whole idea is that we are not separate from nature; we are a part of it. Nature is inspirational and buildings should inspire people, all buildings. I like to say that a building should be like a woman. In other words, architecture should be nurturing, comforting, and protecting everyone who enters the space.

Portrait: Douglas Cardinal (photo by Yousuf Karsh © Douglas Cardinal)
Above: Douglas Cardinal, St. Mary's Church, Red Deer, Alberta, Canada, 1968 (photo by Hubert Hohn © Douglas Cardinal)

Portrait: James Carpenter (photo © JCDA) **Above:** JCDA, Sky-Reflector-Net,
Fulton Center (Grimshaw), New York, USA, 2014 (photo © Alex Fradkin)

"I Like When Architecture Turns into a Lens"

Light in architecture can be taken for granted or it can be controlled, refined, and celebrated. In a way, that alone could be a mission of an architect. What is your view?

Such qualities as transmission and reflection of light can be fully and totally controlled. We can achieve virtually any level of filtration or play of light by combining glass, coatings, and various additives between layers of glass. Our task is to pick or invent appropriate types and combinations of glass to achieve any desirable effect. My interest in glass was always about light and imagery projected on glass. I was always fascinated by remarkable events that occur in nature and how do you take that phenomenon and synthesize that idea and make people experience a similar sensation in a more mindful way? One of my personal most memorable experiences is of being on the ocean in a boat, surrounded by millions of squid at night. It is like the whole ocean lights up.

Manipulating sunlight is one of the major topics that has been stirring the minds of architects since ancient times. From the Roman Pantheon and sculptural pediments of Greek temples to grotesque sculptures by Bernini, architecture has been aiming at new dimensions. For me architecture is something that does not try to be like anything else. I like when architecture turns into a lens, a microscope, a tool of making the beauty of the world clearer, and more experiential.

In conversation with
James Carpenter, Designer

Designer's JCDA studio in
Manhattan, New York, USA,
March 30, 2007

B. 1949 in Washington, D.C., USA;
Lives and practices in
New York, USA

Light as a Transporter
of Information
Articulating Optical
Opportunities
Reflection and
Refraction
Translucency
Luminosity

"I Failed to Be an Artist but I Became an Artistic Architect"

In conversation with
Yung Ho Chang of
Atelier FCJZ, Architect

Atelier FCJZ in Beijing, China,
November 28, 2018

B. 1956 in Beijing, China;
Lives and practices in
Beijing, China

Independent Thinking
Reject Comfort Zone
Autonomous Project
Intelligence
Discovery

You said, "I believe architecture is something down to earth, and ultimately relates to how people live." Tell me you were kidding when you said that because it seems to me that your architecture is anything but down to earth. Down to earth is something that we tend not to notice, right?

Well, maybe something was lost in translation from Chinese. [Laughs.] What I meant is that architecture is tangible. It is about our physical world. Architecture for me is about enjoying life. It is about the way we live. And for us architecture is so much more than just buildings. We design furniture, industrial products, clothing, jewelry, everything. I was even asked to design a cake! It is very simple for me—if I don't know an answer, I search for it. Ignorance is our strength! [Laughs.] I am a risk-taker. Here in China, we started to do good work collectively. But, in a way, good work is not enough. It is important to work outside of one's own comfort zone. Maybe you fail. Maybe you are not going to produce something pretty. But it is necessary to challenge yourself.

To me architecture is not about ideology. Architecture is an autonomous project. It is about making a building with intelligence and wisdom. Architects have a core knowledge that they can offer to the society to make people's lives better. If I had an opportunity, I would make a whole city a better place. And where does a building end? Where does a city begin? I don't think the world of architecture should be divided into East and West. I want to think of it as divided into north and south, climatically, not culturally.

My ideas are both conceptual and formal. I am very much influenced by artists such as Marcel Duchamp and Kazimir Malevich. I am working on [the] ideas of bringing abstract painting into architecture. Meaning, I want to explore such qualities as a brush stroke and paint texture. I am using these ideas to exaggerate or compress spaces. I like to think that I failed to be an artist, but I became an artistic architect.

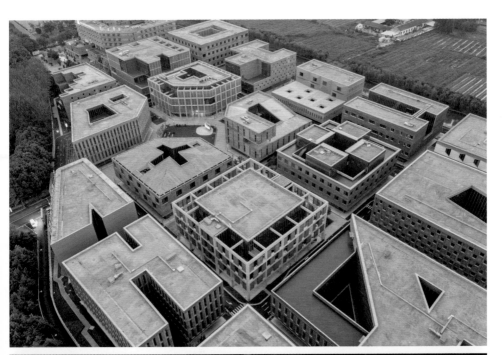

Portrait: Yung Ho Chang (photo © Fangfang Tian) **Above:** Atelier FCJZ, Jiading Mini-Block, Shanghai, China, 2020 (photo © Fangfang Tian) **Bottom:** Atelier FCJZ, Vertical Glass House, Shanghai, China, 2013 (photo © Fangfang Tian)

Portrait: Jeanne-Claude and Christo in front of *Running Fence*, California, USA, 1976 (photo by Wolfgang Volz © 1976 Estate of Christo V. Javacheff) **Top:** Christo and Jeanne-Claude, *The Umbrellas*, Japan, 1984–91 (photo by Wolfgang Volz © 1991 Estate of Christo V. Javacheff) **Bottom:** Christo and Jeanne-Claude, *The Umbrellas*, USA, 1984–91 (photo by Wolfgang Volz © 1991 Estate of Christo V. Javacheff) **Following pages:** Christo and Jeanne-Claude, *Wrapped Reichstag*, Berlin, West Germany, 1971–95 (photo by Wolfgang Volz © 1995 Estate of Christo V. Javacheff)

"We Create Works of Art, Joy, and Beauty"

Is your work about wrapping or is it more about fabric itself? Why did you choose fabric to become a continuous quest for your exploration?

C: First, all our projects are temporary works of art. This is the essential part of our work and that is our esthetical decision. And the uniqueness of our work is that we will never do the same project again. In other words, there will be never again another *Umbrella* project, another *Surrounded Islands*, another *Wrapped Reichstag*, and so on. Each project has a unique proposition. In the mid-1950s I experimented with wrinkled and lacquered surfaces in my paintings. Then I started wrapping very ordinary objects, such as bottles, boxes, furniture, toys, and piles of magazines, and so on. I was fascinated by transformation of objects by simply wrapping them with fabric and plastic. I was intrigued by the idea of missing presence. A very important part of our projects is the fragility of material. All of our projects are very light, they are very nomadic. We try to transform the site through the use of cloth. The fabric is the translator of the flickering experience that will go away. All these projects are very dynamic and are always in motion. Unlike stone sculptures they follow every movement of the wind.

JC: And the color is constantly changing as well. Usually people ask us: "Why do you wrap things?" But you are right, it has to do more with fabric than wrapping. The fabric is like the second skin. Of course, we are not the first artists to use fabric. Egyptians, Romans, and Renaissance artists used fabric as well [Jeanne-Claude points to a postcard of a mural by Giotto]. But we are using real fabric, not in stone, marble, or bronze. And if you ask, "Why our projects attract attention?" Because they are very beautiful, and people need beauty. We create works of art, joy, and beauty. Also, the temporary character of these projects makes people come fast. If I told you, "Look, there is a rainbow over there." You would never say, "I will look at it tomorrow." People need something that is unique in the world. Christo and I are very touched by the expressions: "once in a lifetime" and "once upon a time."

In conversation with Christo Vladimirov Javacheff and Jeanne-Claude Denat de Guillebon, known as Christo and Jeanne-Claude, Artists

Artists' home and studio, SoHo in Manhattan, USA, April 16, 2004

Christo: B. 1935 in Gabrovo, Bulgaria; Lived in Manhattan, USA
D. 2020 in Manhattan, USA
Jeanne-Claude: B. 1935 in Casablanca, Morocco; Lived in Manhattan, USA
D. 2009 in Manhattan, USA

Freedom Is the Enemy of Possession
The Art of Interference!
People Need Beauty
Expedition
Nomadic

"The Constructivists Tried to Break with All Conventions"

In conversation with Jean-Louis Cohen, Historian and Curator

Institute of Fine Arts, New York University, New York, USA, September 18, 2007

B. 1949 in Paris, France; Lives in Paris, France; teaches in New York, USA

Science and Revolution
Transnational History
Avant-garde
Politics
Russia

How would you define the significance of Russian constructivist architecture and what could you say about some of the pioneers of this movement?

Beginning around 1921, the constructivists tried to break with all conventions. However, I wouldn't call their architecture completely nihilistic. For example, Moisei Ginzburg was looking at Le Corbusier's machine metaphors and shared his interest in mathematical proportions. Konstantin Melnikov was an extraordinarily talented and original architect, to be compared with Frank Lloyd Wright. He was not a constructivist or a rationalist, but a very personal and unique inventor of poetic expressionist forms who had a great sense and feeling for monumentality and texture. He understood very well the construction materials at hand and, unlike some other architects who dreamed of constructing buildings in glass and steel in a context where only brick was widely available, he used ordinary materials and modest technologies in the most inventive ways. He looked at Russian vernacular architecture for inspiration, but mostly relied on his own free-wheeling imagination.

What was new and interesting about these architects is the articulation of form and the idea of social transformation on a level that is much more radical than in the West. Modernism, of course, was not happening only in Russia. Moreover, the new programs were not invented from scratch. For example, the workers' clubs were modeled on people's houses (*narodnye doma*), which existed before the revolution, echoing similar programs in France, Italy, England, or Belgium. Many ideas that existed in Europe before 1917 took an extreme form in Russia between 1925 and 1932. This was a remarkable period of condensation and absorption of radical and ambitious thinking and ideas.

Constructivist buildings are the integral part of the identity of our civilization. They have become a part of our cultural, historical, and even emotional heritage. Show me those architects who are practicing today and who can build something more refined and socially meaningful than buildings by Melnikov, Ginzburg, or Ilya Golosov.

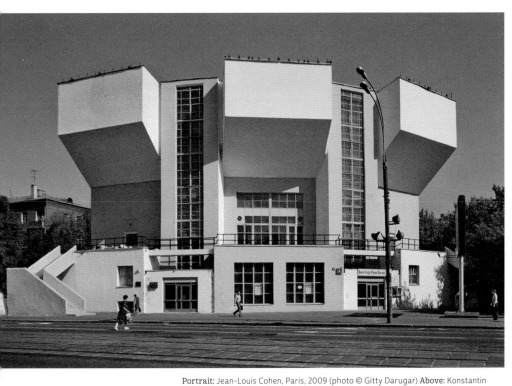

Portrait: Jean-Louis Cohen, Paris, 2009 (photo © Gitty Darugar) **Above:** Konstantin
Melnikov, Rusakov Workers Club, Moscow, Russia, 1927 (photo © Richard Pare)

Portrait: Odile Decq (photo © Franck Juery) **Above:** Studio Odile Decq, Banque
Populaire de l'Ouest, Rennes, France, 1990 (photo © Stephane Couturie)

"I Like Possibilities to Go Faster"

You said you are inspired not just by architecture, but technology, and more specifically—cars, boats, and planes. How do these machines influence you?

All these things help us move and travel faster. That's the reason I love them. Watching documentaries on cars was always fascinating to me. What I really like is speed. I am also fascinated by fighter jets. I am not fond of static places. So, I always think about how my body will experience the space. That's why I am interested in total design and I am particularly inspired by Maison de Verre in Paris by Pierre Chareau. When people visit my buildings, I want them to be free and experience their moment inside. Moving through beautiful spaces, hopefully, will make people forget the worries of their everyday lives.

What I like to address is nondirect. I look for other ways. I like watching how people cross public squares. Everybody likes shortcuts, without even thinking about that. It is the most natural thing in the world. I take shortcuts all the time because I like possibilities to go faster and to experiment with alternatives. I always try to show people the most unexpected ways of perceiving spaces. I love ambiguities that spaces may present. I love when spaces unfold gradually, and you don't understand everything right away. I love when perception has multiple meanings and layers.

This is my way of discovering architecture—I listen to my clients, and I propose something they were often not expecting. All my clients know that they will always be surprised. What I enjoy most is to work on a kind of project that I have never done before, in a place that I have never been before.

In conversation with
Odile Decq, Architect

Architect's hotel in Venice, Italy,
November 24, 2019

B. 1955 in Laval, France;
Lives, practices, and teaches
in Paris, France

Architecture Is Still
a Fight
My Buildings Are Spicy
Create a New Century
The World Is Too Slow
Take a Position

"There Is Architecture That Becomes a Building and There Is Architecture That Refines an Idea"

In conversation with
Thomas Demand, Artist

Zoom video call between
New York, USA, and artist's studio
in Berlin, Germany, May 3, 2021

B. 1964 in Munich, Germany;
Lives and works in Berlin,
Germany and Los Angeles, USA;
teaches in Hamburg, Germany

Collective Memories
Strangely Familiar
Looking Carefully
Complete Control
Timeless Quality

You once said, "I find it interesting to work with architecture that is not about building, but about the process and how you find the form." What are you looking for when you work with architectural models?

What I am after is to explore the power of images. There is architecture that becomes a building and there is architecture that refines an idea. That idea is much closer to art than a building with all the expected conventional functions. I enjoy exploring ideas when they are still fluid. For example, many of the models I found at the Tokyo office of SANAA will never be built. The architects [Kazuyo Sejima and Ryue Nishizawa] play with pure shapes and ideas that may become something or may not. But it is amazing to see all their models and fragments right next to each other. This creates an internal abstract language of communication that has its own power and beauty, and it feeds the architects in their design evolution. I like these explorations for their abstractness. But once you give them to the client, in order to be convincing, you need to insert a human figure to give them a scale. But what I like about architectural models is their potential of suggesting forms without being too explicit and literal. It is the opposite of my own models, which are super calculated and about the biography of the space, and less about the space itself. What I am always looking for is something that is there already. It is about reassurance of things. There is a quote by Saint Augustine, *Illuc ergo venit ubi erat* (He came to a place where he was already). The core of my work is about a very simple operation—looking at the picture, diving in, and trying to see what's in the picture. Good art must have that quality—to slow you down, open up your thoughts, and let you experience it fully, instead of just looking at it. So, an image can make you realize that it is something that you already knew. My work is strangely familiar.

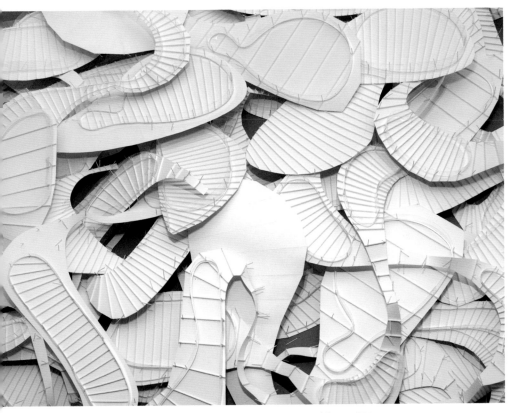

Portrait: Thomas Demand (photo © Brigitte Lacombe) **Above:** Foundation 56, *Framed Pigment Print*,
185.5 x 238 cm, Architectural Models by SANAA (photo © Thomas Demand)

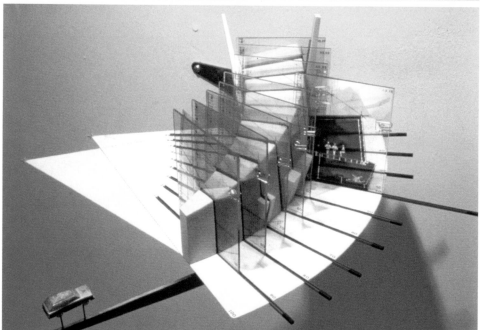

Portrait left: Liz Diller (photo © Geordie Wood) Portrait right: Ric Scofidio (photo © Geordie Wood) Top: Diller Scofidio + Renfro, Blur Building, on Lake Neuchâtel, Switzerland, EXPO 2002, 6th Swiss national exposition (photo © Beat Widmer) Bottom: Diller Scofidio + Renfro, Slow House, Long Island, New York, USA, 1990, project (photo courtesy Diller Scofidio + Renfro) Following pages: Diller Scofidio + Renfro, Institute of Contemporary Art, The ICA, Boston, USA, 2006 (photo © Iwan Baan)

"Making Problems Is More Fun; Solving Problems Is Too Easy"

Álvaro Siza recently told me, "I don't solve problems. I go around them." You don't solve problems either, right?

LD: [Laughs.] Making problems is more fun; solving problems is too easy. Every time we are handed a program, we tear it apart and we continuously ask new questions. Nothing is fixed. In our projects we critique architecture's relevance to the world that it is a part of. That's why so many conventions of our discipline have to be shaken up.

RS: My criticism is that so many architects too quickly fall into accepting certain organizational rules on constructing space without question. Aiming to solve problems means you already know what they are. But we like to explore new territories. This means that some things get resolved properly and some things remain questionable. This produces a richer vocabulary for architecture. We try to avoid labels and we don't take professional boundaries seriously. That's what allows us to continue to question and critique everything we do. We are neither architects doing art nor artists doing architecture. I find that problem-solving alone can become so pragmatic and deadly for architecture because it should be all about questioning. And maybe the first question to ask should be whether the problem at hand should be solved at all or is it enough? To me problem-solving is too limiting and not interesting. Architecture was never just about that.

In conversation with Liz Diller and Ric Scofidio of Diller Scofidio + Renfro, Architects

Architects' studio in Manhattan, New York, USA, January 5, 2016

Liz Diller: B. 1954 in Łódź, Poland; Lives in New York, USA
Ric Scofidio: B. 1935 in New York, USA; Lives in New York, USA

Turning Views On and Off
Publicness/Privateness
Remove All Labels!
Culturally Coded
Politics of Space

"I Believe in Questions That Are Eternal"

In conversation with Dong Gong of Vector Architects, Architect

Architect's office in Beijing, China, December 11, 2018

B. 1972 in Beijing, China;
Lives, practices, and teaches in Beijing, China and Turin, Italy

Boundary—Beyond Boundary

Limitation—Beyond Limitation

Ephemeral and Metaphysical

Atmospheric Harmony

Intangibles

You compare your design process to a chemical reaction. What are the key ingredients that you rely on from project to project?

Every project is a painful process to me. Because when you just start there are so many unknowns—you don't know enough about the site, program, and you don't have enough imagination about the potential spatial qualities. So, it is bits and pieces of issues that are in front of you. For me the only way to find a solution is to spend time sketching and modeling one option after another. It is easy to think about architecture as a creation of physical objects. But there is no end to it. You cannot finish architecture. Architecture will keep growing by itself; it will age, change use, and so on. Architecture never reveals itself. Something else is always revealed through it. The most powerful architecture is never about itself but what you can observe through it. What can space connect you to? The spirit, power, and meaning of architecture should be felt by people.

My Seashore Chapel project seems to be a very simple object. But it was very hard to achieve. We did three distinctly different schemes—complete with many sketches and models. But usually, after these many weeks of struggling there is a moment when all questions and issues dissipate, and one particular design emerges. When that happens, that's what I call that chemical reaction. My work is about testing ideas. I don't get distracted with inspirations.

Now I am asking deeper questions and I try to stretch my abilities to create architecture. I don't have confidence to say that my work is progressing, but my architecture has been transforming. I am consciously throwing away what I already know or what I am very good at. Being too comfortable and sure of what you do is dangerous. I think artists do their best work when they are searching, when they struggle. A good building should provide a feeling of intimacy. It is important not to go too far and not to turn a building into a spectacle. I think the important question is this—what is the problem? I believe in questions that are eternal. I believe the issues we need to address are fundamental—it is about our body, scale, physical limitations, and senses.

Portrait: Dong Gong (photo courtesy Vector Architects) **Top:** Vector Architects, Seashore Chapel, Aranya development, Qinhuangdao, Hebei Province, China, 2015 (photo © Chen Hao) **Bottom:** Vector Architects, Yangshuo Sugar House Hotel on the Li River near Guilin, China, 2017 (photo © Su Shengliang)

Portrait: Balkrishna Doshi (photo © Vinay Panjwani, Vastushilpa Foundation, India) **Above:** Balkrishna Doshi in collaboration with M.F. Husain, Amdavad Ni Gufa art gallery, Ahmedabad, India, 1994 (photo © Vastushilpa Foundation, Ahmedabad)

"Architecture Is a Path That No One Else Has Traveled Before to Get to a New Vista"

In the 1989 letter to your three daughters you said, "Break away from all the rules—forget history books. Go back to your inner perceptions. See things as if you are noticing them for the first time. Only then you will be able to do something of your own." Why do you think it is important to keep reinventing architecture continuously again and again?

I think we always fall in a trap of familiarity, conventions, general opinions, and public considerations. And I think those are the issues that we always get influenced by and we want to do something similar. The same is in architecture. What is architecture? Is the Indian Institute of Management in Bangalore not architecture because it is not simply a building? It is a procession, in which you are experiencing things. The word architecture itself is a trap. So, when we think of architecture, we think of what is common, what is familiar. If something is appreciated by others why not follow the path, right? But to me architecture is a path that no one else has traveled before to get to a new vista.

When I went to work for Le Corbusier in Paris, I was still very young, and I learned many things from him fresh. There was no one style or one theory at his office. Look at the vast difference between his Chandigarh's Capitol complex buildings and Ronchamp chapel, or his houses. That's the main lesson I took from him—there are many ways. I think when there is a rhythm, when there is a pause, when there is a sense of proportion, and when these things are all put together, they make up a synthesis and they sing together. They rhyme together. Then you let all these beautiful qualities unfold one after another. It is like a beautiful dance. Le Corbusier's buildings are made of forms, light, and space, and fluidity.

Look at children—how they go everywhere to discover something and then enjoy it. But gradually we accept such ideologies and conventions that if everyone doing something or likes something than it must be good for us as well. I think the moment you are a child you are free. The moment you are a grown up you get a lot of baggage.

In conversation with
Balkrishna Doshi, Architect

Zoom video call between
New York, USA and Ahmedabad,
India, October 28, 2020

B. 1927 in Pune, India;
Lives and practices in
Ahmedabad, India

A Rhythm, a Pause, a
Sense of Proportion

Narrating Stories,
Events, and Images

Familiar and Surprising

School Without Doors

Our Own Beginning

"Architecture Does Not Answer Questions; It Asks Questions"

In conversation with
Peter Eisenman, Architect

Architect's studio in Manhattan,
New York, USA, February 18, 2016

B. 1932 in Newark, New Jersey,
USA; Lives, practices, and teaches
in New York and New Haven,
Connecticut, USA

Displacement and
Deconstruction
Metaphysical Signifier
Self-Referential
Deep Structure
Figure/Ground

Could you explain Alberti's role in defining theoretical boundaries of architecture and your statement that he was the first architect who conceptualized the idea of space?

Well, before Alberti no one was theorizing space in architecture. Before Alberti there was just homogeneous space. And he articulated space by introducing heterogeneous space, varied and dynamic, as opposed to static. Heterogeneous space is what makes architecture. Look at the façade of his Palazzo Rucellai in Florence. It comprises two systems: a grid system of columns or pilasters and horizontal entablatures, and a wall-bearing system. So, there is a redundancy there. One system is structural, while the other is just visual. Both systems are active on the façade and not one is more important than the other. Alberti was the first person who said, "A column is a decorative element." Meaning it can be just a residue of the wall. And the wall is what makes space and the column decorates space. So, when you have space between two walls that's homogeneous space. Once you put the column in, it divides the space, which becomes heterogeneous. That's what he meant and that's what he did. Without this device, no matter how complex and biomorphic the space might be, it does not interest me. The column is the key element in any space.

All my architecture is about implications of heterogeneous space. All parts should relate to a whole as all objects in space are bound to one another through universal, mathematic relationships. To me, the idea of architecture is to inhibit the routine nature of being, to introduce a new space and time to disrupt the routine of being. What architecture can do, which no other discipline can, is to relate the body, the mind, and the eye. My architecture means nothing, I want to stop any narrative; but the experience is something else. Architecture does not answer questions; it asks questions. It does not solve problems; it creates problems.

Portrait: Peter Eisenman (photo © Chris Wiley) **Above:** Eisenman Architects, Aronoff Center for Design and Art, Cincinnati, Ohio, USA, 1996 (photo courtesy Eisenman Architects)

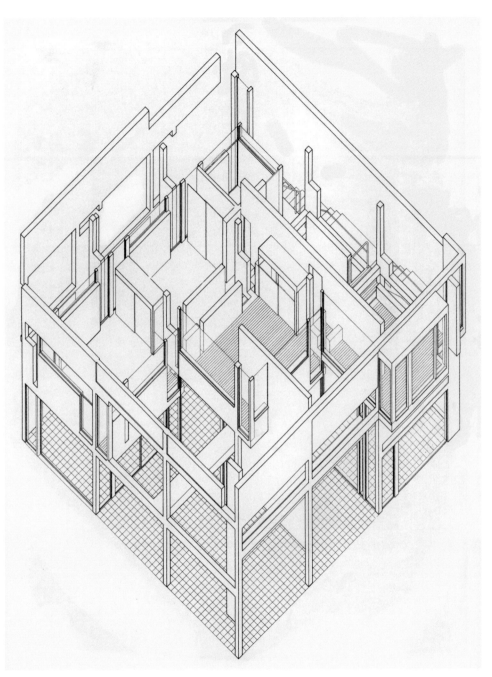

Opposite: Peter Eisenman, Wexner Center for the Visual Arts and Fine Arts Library, Columbus, Ohio, USA, 1989 (photo courtesy Eisenman Architects) **Above:** Eisenman Architects, House II, Hardwick, Vermont, USA, 1970 (isometric drawing courtesy Eisenman Architects)

Portrait: Antón García-Abril and Débora Mesa with Ensamble Studio team at Ca'n Terra, Menorca, Spain (photo © Ensamble Studio)
Above: Ensamble Studio, Hemeroscopium House, Las Rozas Village, Madrid, Spain, 2008 (photo © Roland Halbe)

"We Need an Entirely Different City!"

Could you talk about your idea of using standard, ready-made elements, such as we see here at your Hemeroscopium House, to produce nonstandard results?

In conversation with Antón García-Abril and Débora Mesa of Ensamble Studio, Architects

AG: That's the concept of standardization—to use standard parts that can be assembled into something unique. The new generation, the generation of our students, will not accept standard solutions. We need an entirely different city!

Here we are using weight—these particular beams range from 22 to 25 meters long and weigh 40 to 50 tons each—to reveal the essence of how our spaces are created. We want to celebrate the solidity and enormous weight of the elements we are working with. Architecture is getting thinner and thinner. To hold it together we need very sophisticated mechanisms. But we can get rid of almost everything by using just gravity. When you have these multi-ton elements they stick very well. Here and in other projects we design architecture as unfinished frameworks, which pushes people to assume the responsibility of completing them, to think about what kind of ideal house they would like to live in. Why can't everyone live in an ideal house? To us the ideal house is the unfinished house, in which the home evolves with the residents.

DM: In our work we aim to find the balance between what we need to control and what we do not need to control. We always try to link structure and space in a very essential way. Visiting factories, quarries, or other sites of production is part of the concept design. When we visited a huge precast concrete factory where we happened to come across a cemetery of precast concrete beams that were discarded due to some mistakes in their production. These beams are standard beams engineered for bridges, highways, and aqueducts. So, our first thought was—can we use these beams that no one wants, anyway? We are working with ideas of openness and flexibilities of both spaces and programs.

Architects' home in Las Rozas Village, Madrid, Spain, July 17, 2015

Antón García-Abril: B. 1969 in Madrid, Spain; Lives and teaches in Madrid, Spain and Boston, USA

Débora Mesa: B. 1981 in Madrid, Spain; Lives and teaches in Madrid, Spain and Boston, USA

Nonstandard
Provocative
Incomplete
Fearless
Passion

"Let's Go Over a Sequence of Projects That Represent the Process of Our Skyscrapers' Evolution"

In conversation with
Norman Foster, Architect

Architect's studio in London, UK,
April 15, 2008

B. 1935 in Manchester, UK;
Lives in London, UK; Madrid,
Spain; and Switzerland

Love Affair with Cutting-Edge Technology

Renewable Energy Manifesto

Reinventing a Building Type

Building as an Assembly

Heroic Undertaking

*Could you talk about the anatomy of your skyscrapers,
perhaps as a progression from your first bank tower in Hong
Kong and leading to the latest super-tall skyscraper being
planned in Moscow, the over 600-meter-high Russia Tower?*

Let's go over a sequence of projects that represent the
process of our skyscrapers' evolution. The Hong Kong Bank
[1979] was the first building to question the center core
model of a skyscraper. I still find it extraordinary that this
was the first attempt in the history of the skyscraper that
someone questioned and dissolved the center core and
moved it to the edges. This is what Louis Kahn had done in
his Richards Medical Research Laboratories in Philadelphia,
essentially a low-rise building, where he clearly articulated
"served" and "servant" spaces. So, once you move solid
servant elements—elevators, stairs, airshafts, and so on—to
the sides you have greater potentials for served floor voids
and the ability to break down uniformity vertically to create
interruptions in terms of double-height spaces, which
could then work as refuge floors in the event of a fire. That
thought was developed further in the unbuilt Millennium
Tower in Tokyo [1989] and then through the Commerce Bank
in Frankfurt [1997], which started the spiral organization
and the idea of triangulation explored in the Barcelona
Communication Tower [1992].

And then the 14 Spiraling Gardens in the Swiss Re Tower
[2004] in London is next in this sequence. But when you get
into a new scale, the aspect ratio of a tower changes. In
other words, a pyramid is much more stable than a needle.
In a way, the shift in the Moscow Tower was to persuade
the client to do a single-phase tower instead of a cluster of
three buildings. So, if you put those three buildings together
you will get a tower, which is visually wonderfully slim. Its
aspect ratio is close to a pyramid, like a tripod, which is
incredibly triangularly rigid and stable.

90

Portrait: Norman Foster (photo © Carolyn Djanogly) **Above:** Foster + Partners, Russia Tower
for Moscow City development, Moscow, Russia, 2006, project (rendering © Foster + Partners)

Portrait: Alex Fradkin (photo © Ayla Tagore) **Top:** Todd Saunders of Saunders Architecture, Squish Studio, Fogo Island, Newfoundland, Canada, 2011 (photo © Alex Fradkin, 2014) **Bottom:** Cecil Balmond, *H_edge*, Tokyo, Japan (photo © Alex Fradkin) **Following pages:** MVRDV, Tianjin Binhai Library, Tianjin, China, 2017 (photo © Alex Fradkin)

"Looking for a Moment That Inspires a Sudden Intensity of Being"

Is there one assignment or project that enriched you as an artist? How has it influenced your career?

Early in my architectural photography career, Cecil Balmond gave me some advice when photographing his art installation *H_edge*, in Tokyo that still deeply resonates with me today. He asked me to simply dream and "listen to the music" when photographing his works. Like many of his designs that I have gone on to photograph around the world, Cecil's projects and art installations are very tactile, experiential, and sensory. I interpreted Cecil's advice to be an invitation to relax my preconceptions of what architectural photography *should* look like, and rather, concentrate on what it *could* look like, by focusing on the experience and inherent emotions of space and place.

Similar to my early conversations with Cecil Balmond, one of my great joys in photography is to take the time to study and be in conversation with the architect prior to the shoot. It is a collaboration that always provides considerable insight into the various elements and design inspirations for the finished works—a chance to see into some of the great creative and brilliant minds of our times. This becomes a departure point from where I slow down and allow myself to simply experience the place, its moods over time, light, and seasonal weather conditions. It's a kind of surrender to playfulness and wonderment, where I allow a process of *listening, seeing,* and ultimately *feeling* the experience of architecture. It is all about finding that poetic moment, when light, form, planning, and serendipity all come together. It is all about looking for a moment that inspires a sudden intensity of being.

In conversation with
Alex Fradkin, Photographer

Author's apartment in Long Island City, New York, USA, January 13, 2021

B. 1966 in Los Angeles, USA; Lives in Brooklyn, New York, USA; works around the world

Surrendering to Wonder and Curiosity
Architecture as If People Mattered
Transcendent Spaces and Places
Dream, Create, Feel
The Poetics of Light

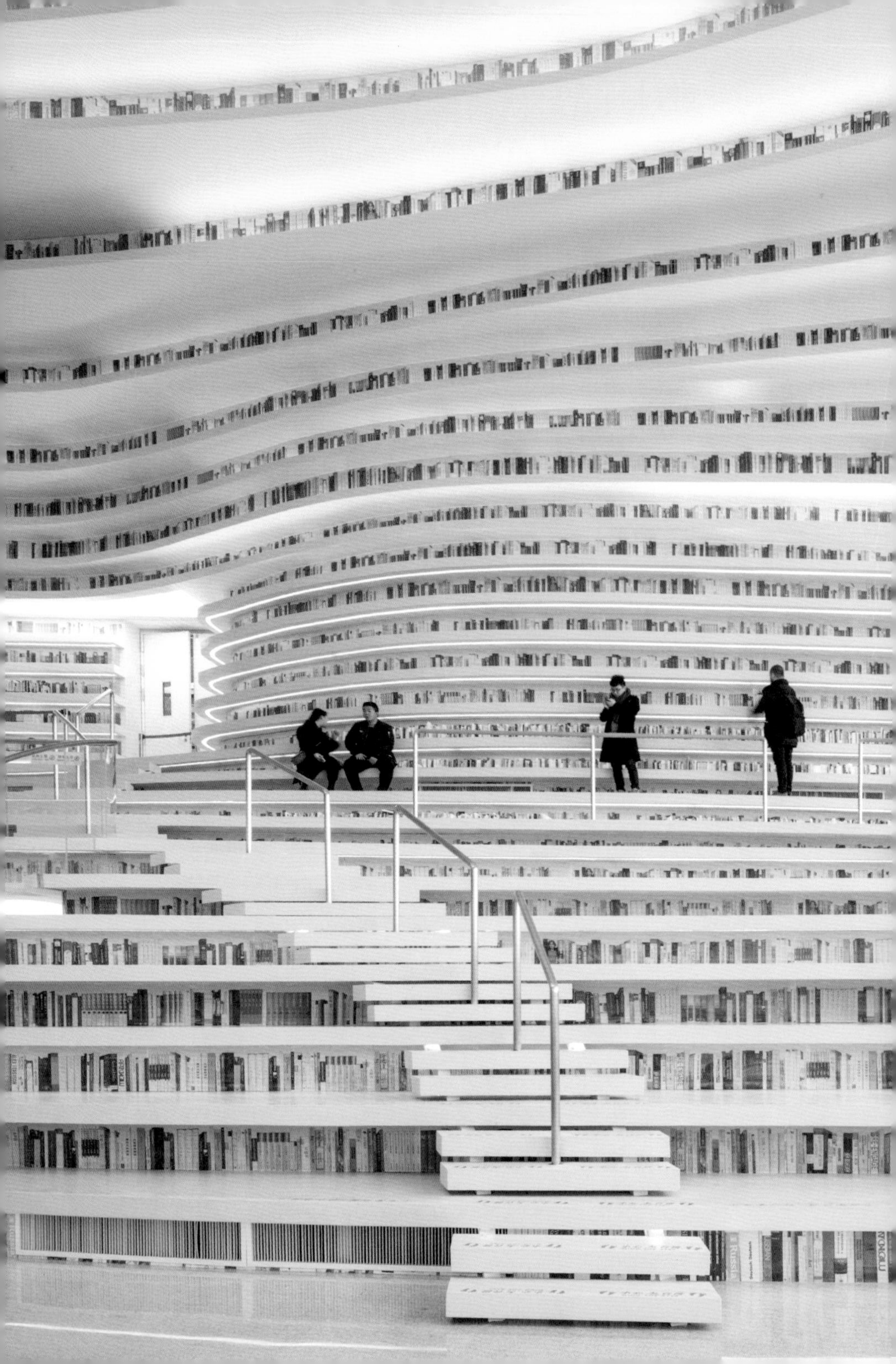

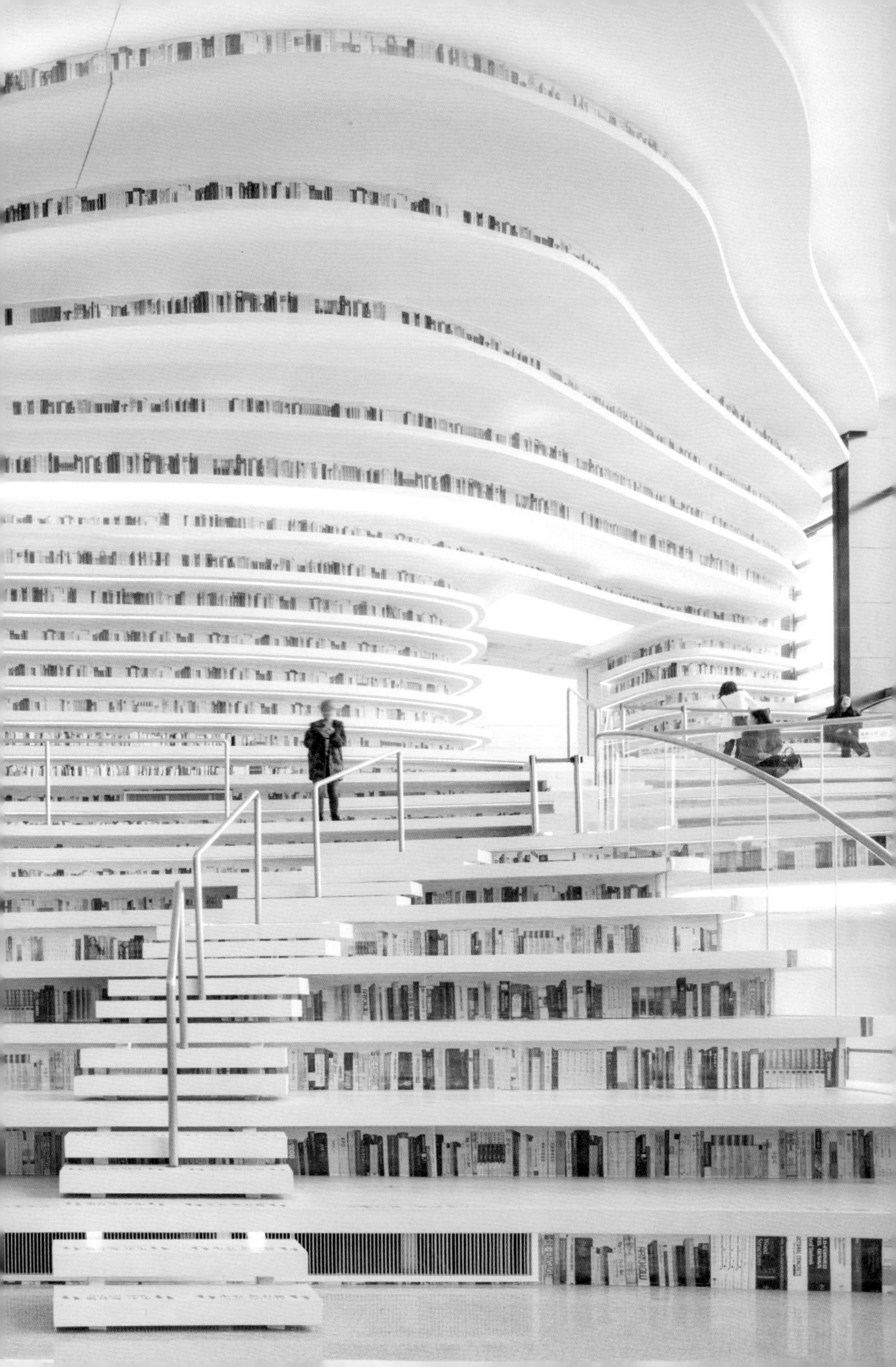

"Architecture Should Be About the Social Project"

In conversation with
Kenneth Frampton,
Historian and Critic

Historian's apartment in
Manhattan, New York, USA,
July 7, 2009

B. 1930 in Woking, UK;
Lives and teaches in
New York, USA

Tectonic as a Poetic of
Construction

Direct Engagement with
Power

Toward Critical
Regionalism

Vision of the Radiant City

Environmental
Argument

What should be architects' fundamental concerns and what one architect would you nominate as exemplary?

In a way, it all begins in France in the middle of the seventeenth century. The purpose of its Académie Royale d'Architecture was to train architects to build the buildings of the State. Otherwise, all the rest was constructed by builders. So, the role of architecture was to serve and represent France's public institutions. I still believe that this should be the primary role of architecture today. Although we live in the world of triumphant capitalism where the primary client is the developer who is building primarily for profit. Clearly, architecture should be about the social project. There is a wonderful aphorism by Walter Benjamin: "Architecture is mostly appreciated by an ordinary person in a state of distraction." It is true. I think there is not enough effort made to educate the public about environmental culture, including architecture. In fact, it is preferable from the point of view of power to keep people in a state of ignorance because late capitalism doesn't like to have restrictions from the environmental standpoint.

One architect that interests me a great deal is Renzo Piano. I wrote a book *Studies of Tectonic Culture*. Piano appears in the book and I have written many times on his work in a rather positive way. He impresses me much more than, for example, Norman Foster and Richard Rogers. They all could be loosely categorized as high-tech architects, but the expressive range of Piano is much greater than that of the other two architects. His capacity to build in relation to different climates and landscapes is quite special. I would particularly touch on his Tjibaou Cultural Center because of its unsentimental rather than monumental reference to native hut of Kanak people in the design of so-called cases (case is a hut in French) that contain public elements: dance studios, exhibition spaces, multimedia library, cafeteria, conference and lecture halls, and are integrated into the low-rise continuous matrix of other parts of the Center. It is a very impressive project because of its relation to the local culture, landscape, vegetation, building traditions, etc.

Portrait: Kenneth Frampton (photo © Alex Fradkin) **Above:** Renzo Piano Building Workshop,
Jean-Marie Tjibaou Cultural Center, Nouméa, New Caledonia, 1998 (photo © John Gollings)

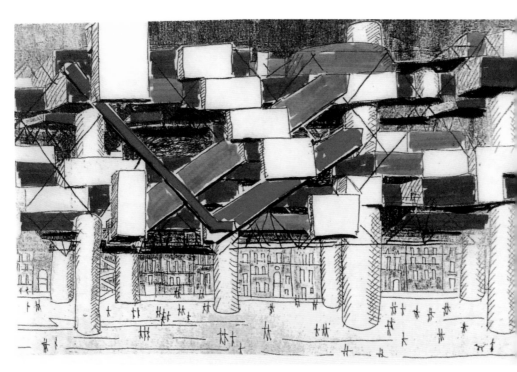

Portrait: Yona Friedman (photo © Paul Almasy, 1974, courtesy akg-images) **Above:** Yona Friedman, the Pompidou Centre, 1970, competition entry, drawing in multicolor markers and black ink on white paper (drawing © Yona Friedman)

"Imagine, Having Improvised Volumes 'Floating' in Space, Like Balloons!"

I was just at the Pompidou Centre with its glorious colors—blue for air, yellow for electricity, green for water, and red for circulation. And I saw your proposal for Ville Spatiale on display there. What about your own 1970 competition entry for the Centre?

In my competition entry, I had to propose a façade, but I did not have ONE; I had twenty or more. The Ville Spatiale is not supposed to have one specific façade. Its volume disposition and façades change continuously. So, our projects are very different. As built, the project by Piano and Rogers is not about flexibility. Every floor is a large "shoebox" with defined contour and levels. If you take any tower, every floor is the same. Only the arrangement of partitions and furniture is different. But I am looking for techniques that will enable people a trial-and-error planning process where nothing is completely fixed or fixed very minimally. Everything needs to be tested and improved all the time. Only then, architecture can be called truly mobile. I insist that I introduced a new idea in architecture; it is called improvisation. That is completely contrary to architectural education, which is about building for eternity. My Pompidou Centre was to be a continuous improvisation.

The Ville Spatiale proposes empty "space," with no general enclosure, no definite floors, walls, floors, and ceilings. Anything that's predetermined is questionable. Space-frame structure, a minimal one, is envisioned as an antigravity device simply for hanging volumes freely imagined by the users. Why "pollute" earth with buildings? The user-self planner can install anything, even a tower into the grid. Imagine, having improvised volumes "floating" in space, like balloons!

In conversation with
Yona Friedman, Architect

Architect's apartment in Paris, France, October 19, 2015

B. 1923 in Budapest, Hungary; Lived and practiced in Paris, France
D. 2020 in Los Angeles, USA

Unpredictable and Unexpected
Freedom to the Inhabitant
Randomness in Order
Mobile Elements
Self-Planning

"One Day All the Dreamers Will Get Together to Build a Fantastic World"

In conversation with
Massimiliano and
Doriana Fuksas, Architects

Architects' hotel on 57th Street
in Manhattan, New York, USA,
April 5, 2019

Massimiliano Fuksas: B. 1944 in
Rome, Italy; Lives and practices
in Rome, Italy and Paris, France

Doriana Fuksas: B. 1955 in Rome,
Italy; Lives and practices in
Rome, Italy and Paris, France

Architecture as a
Narrative, as a Painting

Architecture Is the Art
of Forgetting

Multiplicity of Visions

Intensity of Feelings

Art of Imagination

*You said, "You have to have more dreams for your future
than about the past." In other words, you move on, you look
ahead, right?*

MF: It doesn't matter what dreams you had in the past
and how many were realized. You may have realized one
thousand dreams, but you still need to have a thousand
dreams more. It is all about the future. You can't dream if
you only see what's in front of you now. To move forward
we must change the context. It is all about being able to
feel architecture with all your senses. What is architecture?
We are just about to discover it! I am inspired more by
philosophy than art. We don't care about shapes and
forms. They come and go. Arthur Schopenhauer said,
"Change alone is eternal, perpetual, immortal." So, I don't
start, I continue! I am always drawing and painting. And
then the project comes. I need to be ready for a project to
come at the right moment. I am building up the intensity of
feelings. There is no inspiration; it is about getting ready
to express our emotions to be able to give an expression.
We want to design something that would allow people
to have a dream. And we don't want them to have the
same dreams as ours. We want them to have their own
dreams. The world is for the dreamers. A good building is
something that is capable of becoming something else, a
dream. One day all the dreamers will get together to build
a fantastic world.

DF: Ideas never come out of the blue; you need to look
around and pay attention to how people live. Architecture
should accommodate people, their environments, and
their desires. Architecture is for people; otherwise, it is
a mistake. For us, architecture is the art of forgetting.
Otherwise, you become nostalgic. Every day you have
to forget what you did the day before. The question is—
what is the future? For us now is the future. We work fast
because we want to keep up with our emotions. We need
to make immediate and spontaneous decisions. Otherwise,
there is no energy.

Portrait: Doriana and Massimiliano Fuksas (photo © Gianmarco Chieregat)
Above: Studio Fuksas, Roma Convention Center (The Cloud), Rome, Italy, 2016
(photo © Roland Halbe)

Portrait: Jeanne Gang (photo © Sally Ryan) Above: Studio Gang, Aqua Tower (82 stories), Chicago, Illinois, USA, 2010 (photo by Steve Hall © Hall + Merrick)

"Without an Intellectual Construct, Life Is Boring"

You said that architecture enables us to solve problems in our society. What about such structures as churches, museums, or memorials? Don't we love them for reasons other than solving problems?

Well, our mission is not just to solve problems. Because some things are not a problem. [Laughs.] But I think it is important to be able to problematize projects, not so they can be "solved" but because by posing a question, it makes design more interesting. It can set apart a certain conflict or an issue and help us rethink them. Without an intellectual construct, life is boring. It's important to create tension. I am interested in architecture as a medium we can use to speak about broader issues.

I was always a huge observer of relationships, both between people and between people and their environment. I think of architecture as a system; how you set up various opportunities for people to relate to one another, and to be empowered. What are the opportunities for people to interact? How can buildings spark new relationships? Take our Aqua Tower in Chicago—the form is important, but that's not how the idea was hatched. As a precursor, I was interested in how tall buildings could be more social and less isolating, more specific with respect to their context and less generic. We had a site, which was buried in the city, surrounded by very tall buildings. The initial idea was to create hills and valleys, so to speak, on the façades of the building, so the occupants could see more of the views from the building. But then, how do you inhabit that topography? That prompted the idea of slicing the hills into horizontal layers, and making those exterior spaces into distinct balconies, all of them unique—each shaped and determined by the wind impact and creating spaces for social interaction. There is nothing random about the building's shape.

It is important to me to reveal things. If you look at our work, it is always about revealing structure, revealing materials. Showing how things can be light or lighter. I am very interested in space itself, the relation of light and shadow. The tactile qualities. But first, I see buildings as facilitators of relationships.

In conversation with Jeanne Gang of Studio Gang, Architect

The High Line Park in New York, USA, September 13, 2016

B. 1964 in Belvidere, Illinois, USA; Lives and practices in Chicago, Illinois, USA

Revealing Something
Unexpected
Thought-Provoking
Communicative
People-Centric
Tectonic

"I Have Become a Nomad"

In conversation with
Laurian Ghinițoiu, Photographer,
Architect, and Journalist

Via email correspondence,
January 2021

B. 1985 in Bicaz, Romania;
Currently a nomad; works
around the world

Contiguous Journey
Exposing Inequality
Sense of Belonging
Raise Awareness
Investigation

You are trained as an architect, and it was only after Wolfgang Buttress, an English artist, noticed your photos of his UK Pavilion at the 2015 Expo in Milan that you decided to switch to photography. What was that shifting moment like in your career, and what was it that finally persuaded you to follow your new career path?

Photography was always a passion that I never had enough time for. The feedback received from Wolfgang helped me see it as a tool, a tool that I can use to explore and document the built environment around the world. How can you say NO to that? I thought, "Architecture can wait, at least for now." And it will probably come back into my life, one way or another. What followed was and remains unknown, spontaneous, but also organic and it suits me very well. Without having a strong sense of belonging to any one place I have become a nomad (even now, during the ongoing pandemic). It is through my work as a photographer that I want to examine and document people's living conditions in various places and cultures. Transition, post-occupancy, trauma, global warming, inequality, corruption, and discrimination are among the subjects that I am interested in the most and my photographs, are meant to raise awareness, point to some answers and, why not, pose more questions?!

Portrait: Laurian Ghinițoiu (photo © Laurian Ghinițoiu) **Top:** Lina Ghotmeh & Bernanrd Khoury, Residential Tower, Beirut, Lebanon (damaged in the 2020 Beirut Explosion, August 4, 2020), September 2020 (photo © Laurian Ghinițoiu) **Bottom:** Marble quarry, Eastern Portugal. The extracted marble travels between four factories in Europe before it is shipped to New York, USA, August 2020 (photo © Laurian Ghinițoiu) **Following pages:** Burning Man, an annual nine-day gathering in the Nevada Desert for more than 70,000 people, installation by BIG, August 2018 (photo © Laurian Ghinițoiu)

Portrait: John Gollings, 2014 (photo courtesy John Gollings) **Above:** Vittala Temple, Vijayanagara, India (photo © John Gollings, 1984)

"Every Great Civilization Finally Dies"

I read about your obsession with documenting dead cities that you visited in Asia and in the Middle East. What was it that attracted you there and why do you keep going back?

I generally was asked to visit these unique sites by cultural institutions that needed images for a book or exhibition. What made me return was to explore the sites in more detail or record new discoveries as I became beguiled by the quality of the architecture and planning. However, the important question has to do with the meaning of dead cities. They are a reminder that every great civilization finally dies for a range of reasons. Climate change, war, jealousy, and economics can contribute, but decline is inevitable!

These are large sites and I need to return to document all the ruins. New discoveries and restoration are factors. Plus, I develop connections that have fostered my wisdom and understanding of cultural issues and made me a better person. The architecture there is profound, and it leaves modern work looking immature and flimsy.

My photographs are quite accurate but controlled by composition and lighting to emphasize the design and to give context. I hope the best of these photos transcend the literal and become memorable.

In conversation with
John Gollings, Photographer

Email correspondence,
December 2020

B. 1944 in Melbourne, Australia;
Lives in Melbourne, Australia;
works around the world

Searching for a
Narrative
Meaning of Dead Cities
Fabricating the Truth
Human Intervention
Memorable

Above: Teatro Farnese Parma, Palazzo della Pilotta, Parma, Italy, 1628 (photo © John Gollings, 2012)
Opposite: Fer Kuo Stepwell Village of Vasad Gujurat, India (photo © John Gollings, 2017)

"Architecture That's Not Formulaic Has a Potential to Be Art"

In conversation with
Dan Graham, Amateur Artist

Artist's apartment in Manhattan,
New York, USA, July 31, 2017

B. 1942 in Urbana, Illinois, USA;
Lives in New York, USA

Recreating Childhood
Desires
Pleasure and Humor
Optical Distortions
Time Paradoxes
Playground

What do you think about conceptual art?

You know, I have nothing to do with it! I hate conceptual art. I think it is a fraud … because art should not be about philosophy; that's bullshit. I love Minimal Art—most of all Dan Flavin. I think great art is about addressing stereotypes and clichés … Art is a form of education. You are always going to learn something. I think art should be humorous. Duchamp's work is very funny. Lichtenstein's work is very funny. I am talking about the work itself. The critics are making too much fuss about art. Ideas come from within—if you don't like your decade, you invent your own fantasy, your own utopian decade. Isn't that a fantastic reason for becoming an artist?! You know what I think? Art should be an amateur's hobby, a kind of passionate hobby, that's all. My work is a hobby. My work is about a spectator, not an object. I realized with time that what I really wanted to do was something related to commonplace architecture I observed in the cityscape. That's why I started building my pavilions. Architects should aim to be artists. Buildings should be artistic, playful, and critical. My pavilions are funhouses and critiques of corporate culture. Architecture that's not formulaic has a potential to be art. I always wanted to do hybrid things, what's on the edges and in between of what we expect and what we know. No one knows whether rock music is poetry, performance, theater, or music. My best work is always a collaborative work … The problem with many architects is that they are too busy. They have no time to look at each other's buildings. It is very sad. Otherwise, they would learn how to improve things. Don't you think? [Laughs.] My favorite architect is Itsuko Hasegawa. Her drawings are astonishingly good. Her work has humor. She was the student of Kazuo Shinohara who was very influential in Japan, particularly on such architects as Hasegawa, as well as Toyo Ito and Kazuyo Sejima. Sejima may have been influenced by my work. I always wanted to do hybrid things in between architecture, literature, and landscape architecture.

Portrait: Dan Graham (photo courtesy Dan Graham) **Above:** Dan Graham, pavilion/sculpture for Argonne, Argonne National Library, Chicago, Illinois, 1978 (photo courtesy Dan Graham)

Portrait: Herb Greene at Joyce Residence, Snyder, Oklahoma, 1960 (photo © Robert Alan Bowlby, 1961) **Top:** Herb Greene, Prairie House, 1961 (photo © Robert Alan Bowlby; Robert A. Bowlby Collection, American School Archives, University of Oklahoma Libraries) **Bottom:** Herb and Mary Greene, 1961 (photo © Robert Alan Bowlby; Robert A. Bowlby Collection, American School Archives, University of Oklahoma Libraries)

"The Result Was a Kind of Collage to Be Inhabited"

You described your Prairie House as a "wounded creature."
What were some of your inspirations while designing it?

The idea was to relate the house to the prairies and the idea of a dwelling. A wounded creature was one of the inspirational images. I also tried to express the idea of being tied to the earth with a yearning to be free and I used such images as a beast, a buffalo, and a bird taking off. I wanted it to look like different things in one and as a continuous space and surface. I was also influenced by the teachings of philosopher Alfred North Whitehead on perception and interpretation of the visual world. I tried to apply his ideas of a "mental continuum," in which the viewer interprets feelings and imagination from different symbols all within a single image. The result was a kind of collage to be inhabited. The house became nicknamed the "Prairie Chicken House," as it was called in the 1961 *Life Magazine* article that featured the Julius Shulman photographs. He was in the area then to photograph Bruce Goff's famous Bavinger House [1950], also in Norman, Oklahoma. Students told him about my house. Shulman was so impressed that he ended up staying for three days with us. When published, the house became a sort of sensation for a while. People reacted to it as a curiosity and a kind of puzzle. It was the interior that moved everyone the most. We invited people to visit on Sundays, often women would have tears in their eyes. They really enjoyed the space. The so-called eye, a large panoramic window on the second floor faced west to look out onto the prairie.

In conversation with
Herb Greene, Architect
and Artist

Skype conversation between
New York and Berkeley, California,
USA, October 16, 2020

B. 1929 in Oneonta, New York, USA;
Lives in Berkeley, California, USA

Going Against the
Currents
Individual Solutions
Organic Forms
Pure Feeling
Authentic

"When You Layer Things Over Each Other— Some Things Come Up"

In conversation with
Zaha Hadid, Architect

Email correspondence following
multiple face-to-face meetings,
July 2008

B. 1950 in Baghdad, Iraq; Lived
and practiced in London, UK

D. 2016 in Miami Beach,
Florida, USA

A Feeling of Flow and
Movement in Space
Discovering Things for
the First Time
Malevich's Tektonic
Spirit of Adventure
Fluid and Organic

There is a fascinating oil painting Grand Buildings, *set in London's Trafalgar Square. Could you explain how a particular site condition may feed your imagination in creating such paintings? How do such paintings help you to inform and reimagine the actual sites?*

One concrete result of my fascination with Malevich, in particular, was that I took up painting as a design tool. This medium became my first domain of spatial invention. I felt limited by the poverty of the traditional system of drawing in architecture and was searching for new means of representation. It provided me with the tool for intense experimentation in both form and movement that led to our radical approach to developing a new language for architecture. I enjoy painting, and it was always a critique of what was currently available to us at the time as designers. I mean everything was done through plan and section. So, the paintings really came because I thought the projections required a degree of distortion and deformation at the time, but eventually it affected the work itself, of course. The work became much more malleable because the origin of the work was also about overlayering—when you layer things over each other— some things come up.

The idea of these paintings is to attempt to embed an object into the site with a whole series of articulate relationships— trying to draw out features from the context so that in the end there is a sense of "embedded-ness", and "fit-ness" into the context. A project design can change as the research of the site reveals things. An ideal situation is very rare. We've learned to apply new techniques to urbanism. As we've done in our buildings, where elements fit together to form a continuum, which we applied on the scale of whole cities. We can develop a whole field of buildings, each one different, but visually all connected, creating an organic, continually changing, field of highly correlated buildings. Such an approach leads to overall elegant coherence.

Portrait: Zaha Hadid at her London apartment (photo © Alberto Heras)
Above: Zaha Hadid Architects, MAXXI National Museum of XXI Century
Arts, Rome, Italy, 2009 (photo © Roland Halbe)

Above: *Grand Buildings*, Trafalgar Square, London, UK, 1985, project (diptych © Zaha Hadid Foundation)

Portrait: Roland Halbe (photo © Roland Halbe)
Above: Max Núñez, Ghat House, Casa
Guerrero, Zapallar, Chile, 2015 (photo
© Roland Halbe) **Right:** OMA, Fondazione
Prada, Milan, Italy, 2015 (photo © Roland Halbe)
Following pages: Ensamble Studio, SGAE
Headquarters in Santiago de Compostela,
Spain (photo © Roland Halbe)

"There Is a Lot of Psychology and Improvisation in My Approach"

It is interesting to know about the work that goes into documenting a project. I am fascinated by your photos of a wall mockup for SGAE Headquarters in Santiago de Compostela designed by Ensamble Studio, which was assembled at a stone quarry. How was that experience?

Ideally, I like taking walk-throughs with architects before documenting a project. They help me understand architects' thoughts. And I try to read their intentions between the lines; all this information gets memorized and stored subconsciously. There is a lot of psychology and improvisation in my approach.

Shooting the mockup of the SGAE Headquarters wall was fun, as it is always a lot of fun shooting projects for Antón [García-Abril] and Débora [Mesa]. Antón is quite crazy in a positive way and there are always adventures involved, when shooting for him. Nothing is impossible for him, and I know very few people who look at their world with such enthusiasm as he does. We drove to the quarry by car from Madrid. The most remarkable thing of the mockup is that it was done at all. He convinced his client to do a 1:1 scale mockup of such enormous dimensions. We took Antón's son with us and he served as the perfect scale model for me to make the structure look even bigger than it was.

In conversation with
Roland Halbe, Photographer

Via email correspondence,
December 2020

B. 1963 in Karlsruhe, Germany;
Lives in Stuttgart, Germany;
works around the world

Between the Lines
Curiosity
Patience
Lucidity
Balance

"Good Architecture Cannot Be Legal; It Is Illegal!"

In conversation with
Zvi Hecker, Architect

Architect's studio in Berlin, Germany, May 19, 2015

B. 1931 in Kraków, Poland; Lives and practices in Berlin, Germany

Walls, Sunflowers, and Spirals

Tradition and Transformation

Cement, Sand, and Water

Sense of Security

Enclosure

You like testing your clients by exploring your limits, don't you?

You know, Bruce Goff once told me about Wright's reaction to one of his designs: "Bruce, who are you trying to scare?" And then he added, "But we do scare *them* sometimes." [Laughs.] Well, I am an artist after all. You know, real art and real architecture cannot be totally legal; very often both are in direct conflict with legality. For example, look at my Spiral Apartment House in Ramat Gan [Israel]. It has its illegal twist. One can question, for example, the legality of the changes I made in plans during the construction phase, plans that were approved by the building authorities and bought on paper by the people. They wanted to sue me! The construction was stopped repeatedly because of complaints from the neighbors. In order to keep going, it needed the assertion of my personal will and total dedication, by working by myself on the scaffolding. This illegal provocative element is not foreign to art; it is a kind of disruptive agent that upsets the established order.

Well, I don't know what architecture is; I only know what architecture is not. I have to discover it for myself in each new project. You may find some common threads in my work, though it seems to me that I always start from zero. I believe so. For me, designing a building is like cooking a meal. I try not to reheat the old stuff but start with ordinary ingredients in hopes of arriving at an extraordinary taste.

Portrait: Zvi Hecker (photo © Arkadiusz Łuba) **Above left:** Zvi Hecker, Jewish Primary School Berlin (Heinz-Galinski-Schule), Germany, 1993 (drawing courtesy Zvi Hecker, Collection of the Jewish Museum, Berlin) **Above right:** Zvi Hecker, Spiral Apartment House, Ramat Gan, Israel, 1984 (drawing courtesy Zvi Hecker) **Following pages:** Zvi Hecker, Spiral Apartment House, Ramat Gan, Israel, 1984 (photo courtesy Zvi Hecker)

Portrait: Sheila Hicks, Musée Carnavalet, Paris, France, 2018 (photo by Cristobal Zanartu © VG Bild-Kunst)
Above: *SHEILA HICKS: Thread, Trees, River*, MAK Exhibition, 2020 *La Sentinelle de Safran*, 2018 (photo © MAK/Georg Mayer)

"Imagine, Building Architecture With Soft Materials"

No one works with fibers the way you do. There is something architectural about your works. Could you touch on how you discovered your way?

Well, you just have to keep going. So many artists hang up on one little discovery they have made. Then they become *génial* and start repeating themselves forever and ever. But if they just tried to keep going, discovering materials and what you can do with them. That's how art was explored at the Bauhaus. When I went to art schools my art teachers encouraged me to play with all kinds of materials—clay, papier mâché, foam, and so on. I was always interested in discovering things. I am still doing that now. I stay alert about everything. I come across all kinds of machines. Once you try how to use them you discover things you could never imagine. I love Bricolage Art. That's were creativity comes in—when you take something to modify it in another way, add to it, subtract, and adapt to have another function.

Observation is critical. All my work is trial and error. But I am being well aware that most of the time when you try something new you are going to fail. That's OK; you keep going to find how something may work. You know, art does need to work. If you come back to it again and again, as we go back to some classics, that means that art does work.

And about architecture. What is architecture? It is a manmade space modulation. I was lucky to go to Yale at the time when art school, architecture, and art history departments were all in one building. I am fascinated with using a soft material and making it into architecture. Imagine, building architecture with soft materials, creating a new kind of environment—weaving different materials and playing with space, light, shadows, and colors.

In conversation with
Sheila Hicks, Artist

The High Line Park in New York, USA, June 1, 2017

B. 1934 in Hastings, Nebraska, USA; Lives and works in Paris, France

Observation Is Critical
Play with Materials
Space Modulation
Trial and Error
Stay Alert

"I Am Interested in Architecture That Speaks to the Soul"

In conversation with
Steven Holl, Architect

Architect's office in New York,
USA, September 11, 2019

B. 1947 in Bremerton, Washington,
USA; Lives, practices, and teaches
in New York, USA

Natural Light as a
Primary Space-Shaping
Material
Drawing Is a Form of
Thought
Phenomenological Aim
Inspirational Moment
I Am an Idealist!

*In your abstracted buildings, you avoid giving us familiarities
to something that we already know. You want us to figure
them out based on unfamiliar elements, right?*

I think light, space, material, color, details, those are
elements in themselves. And the power of abstraction
is that we can make things in a new way. We can make
new meanings, new entities. We don't need references.
Architecture is art. I believe that architecture can change
the way we live. It can change a person. It can change
the world. I am interested in architecture that speaks
to the soul.

In his 2016 book *Reductionism in Art and Brain Science*,
Columbia University professor Eric Kandel, a Nobel
Prize–winning neuroscientist, argues that the brain
needs abstraction. The internal mechanisms with which
we see and experience visual and physical phenomena,
depend on a bottom-up approach, meaning building
up from elements of abstraction, coming to terms with
something that we analyze and to make sense of it. The
opposite, top-down approach of given figuration stifles
our imagination. A form of a cupola is an example of the
top-down thinking. In other words, we already know
what it is. We have multiple references to what a cupola
is. It is not abstract enough, as the meaning of the thing
is a given, and therefore our mind is not working on
figuring it out.

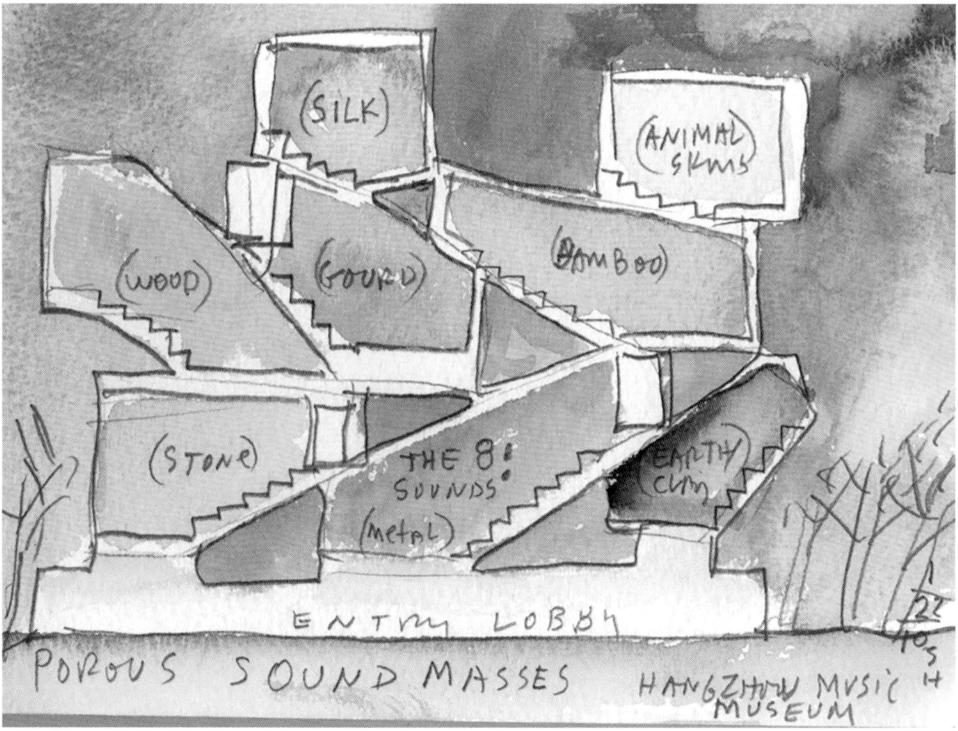
(SILK)
(ANIMAL SKINS)
(WOOD)
(GOURD)
(BAMBOO)
(STONE)
THE 8 SOUNDS
(metal)
EARTH clay
ENTRY LOBBY
POROUS SOUND MASSES
HANGZHOU MUSIC MUSEUM

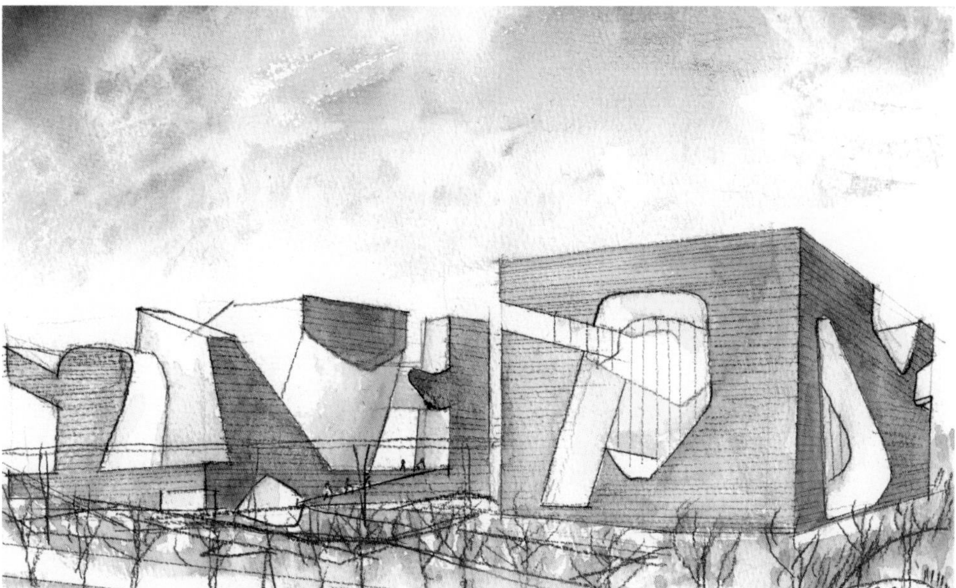

Portrait: Steven Holl (photo © Mark Heitoff) Top: Hangzhou Music Museum, Hangzhou, China, 2008 (watercolor © Steven Holl) Bottom: Tianjin Ecocity Ecology and Planning Museums, China, 2012 (watercolor © Steven Holl) Following pages: "Stone Box with Seven Bottles of Light" conceptual sketch for Chapel of St. Ignatius, Seattle, USA, 1997 (watercolor © Steven Holl)

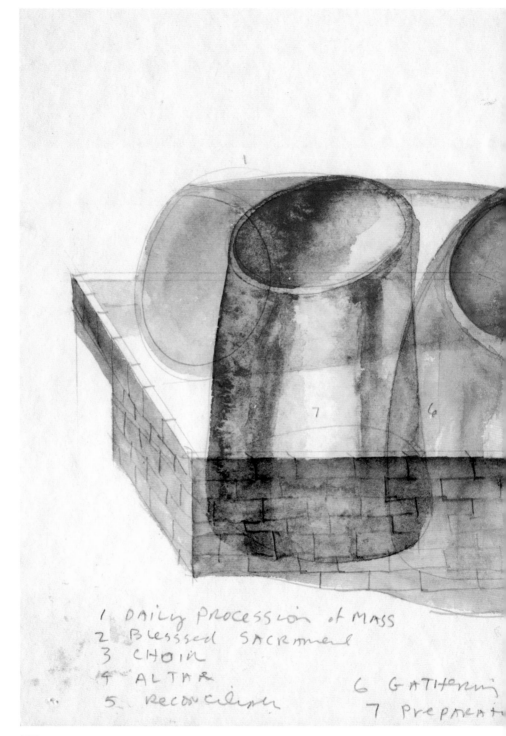

1 DAILY PROCESSION of MASS
2 Blessed Sacrament
3 CHOIR
4 ALTAR
5 Reconciliation

6 GATHERING
7 Preparation

2

3

4

5

CHAPEL OF
ST. IGNATIUS 9/28/94.
S.H.

Portrait: Bjarke Ingels (photo © Ulrik Jantzen) **Above:** BIG, VIA 57 West, New York, USA, 2016 (photo © Alex Fradkin)

"Our Architecture Is Never Shaped by a Single Hand"

You worked for Rem Koolhaas for three years. What did you learn from him?

Koolhaas was a major discovery for me and that's why I wanted to work for him. I can't think of contemporary architecture without him. He is the major force in my education. He taught me not so much about how to design a beautiful building as an isolated object, but how to use architecture as a tool for engaging in development, politics, social structures, and to be free to realize various means of expression. Architecture for him is not about aesthetics. Architecture is not driven by styles, but by ideas. Our architecture is never shaped by a single event, never conceived by a single mind, and never shaped by a single hand. Neither is it the direct materialization of a personal agenda or pure ideals, but rather the result of an ongoing adaptation to the multiple conflicting forces flowing through society. We, architects don't control the city—we can only aspire to intervene. Architecture evolves from the collision of political, economic, functional, logistical, cultural, structural, environmental, and social interests, as well as interests yet unnamed and unforeseen.

In conversation with Bjarke Ingels of BIG, Architect

Restaurant near The Rubin Museum of Art, Manhattan, New York, USA, December 15, 2009

B. 1974 in Copenhagen, Denmark; Lives and practices in New York, USA and Copenhagen, Denmark

Architecture as a Dialogue with Society

Power to Adapt the Environment to Life

Technological Innovations

Future Possibilities

Speculations

"My Intention Is to Free Architecture"

In conversation with
Junya Ishigami, Architect

Architect's office, Tokyo, Japan,
March 12, 2018

B. 1974 in Kanagawa prefecture,
Japan; Lives and practices in
Tokyo, Japan

Architecture Is Not
Free Enough
New Comfortabilities
Blurring Boundaries
New Atmosphere
Loose

*About your table project you said, "I had in mind the idea of
expressing something very gentle, almost like a cloud." Do you
imagine your work as light as a cloud?*

The cloud metaphor may be valid but the main image
I had in mind was the surface of water. I wanted to make
it so thin and light that it would appear floating. The table
installation seems absolutely motionless but if you just
touch it ever so slightly all the plants start swaying, like
swimming in a pond. It was originally designed for a small
restaurant. The client's philosophy is all about serving
very few people but in a very special way. The idea was to
create space for small groups that could enjoy a meal in a
secluded setting. But the space was too tight to introduce
any partitions, so I proposed to define spaces by several
oversized tables. Each table was larger than needed for
each party, so the unoccupied areas were filled with plants
to screen the space for privacy and atmosphere. That
commission led to an installation project, in which I pushed
one of the table's dimensions to extreme. The gallery
space had a narrow entrance, so the idea was to roll the
table to fit it in and unroll it once inside. [Laughs.] So, we
calculated how to distort the table and how it could be
brought back to equilibrium by heavy plants.

My intention is to free architecture by inventing new types
and varieties to give people more options to explore many
more lifestyles. We, architects, try to challenge what we
know. What I am after is a new scenery. I want to bring
the outside inside of my buildings. I am not talking about
dissolving boundaries between inside and outside. I am
talking about bringing the outside environment in, not
literally, but spatially. I don't want anything to dominate,
whether it is structure, space, or furniture. I use them
all equally. There is no hierarchy. Usually architecture is
divided by a wall, but I want to make space that's soft,
ambiguous, flexible, and new. I want to create a new feeling
in architecture—a fusion of space, atmosphere, structure,
and landscape. If I have a chance to change the future,
I want to try it.

Portrait: Junya Ishigami, 2018 (photo © Laurian Ghinițoiu) Top: Junya Ishigami + Associates, Table, aluminum, partly steel, 2005 (photo courtesy Junya Ishigami + Associates); 9.5-meter span, 3mm-thick single aluminum sheet, supporting itself and carrying 700 kilograms of plants Bottom: Junya Ishigami + Associates, Farm Garden "Water garden", Nasushiobara, Japan, 2018 (photo © Laurian Ghinițoiu); 300 trees were replanted to create a new form of nature with water ponds, moss, and stones

Portrait: Toyo Ito (photo © Richard Schulman) **Above:** Toyo Ito & Associates, Architects, Sendai Mediatheque, Aoba-ku, Sendai, Miyagi, Japan, 2000 (photo courtesy Toyo Ito & Associates, Architects)

"Wind and Clouds Inspire My Design"

You once said, "I have one dream—architecture should equal nature. When I start a project, I may dream of a forest clearing, a silent pool of water, or a flowing river." What other visions inspire you and what kind of architecture do you try to pursue?

As you say, I always derive inspirations from forests, trees, and water in nature. In addition to those, natural phenomena such as wind and clouds inspire my design. My Sendai Mediatheque in Japan is often compared to a forest. I wanted to create a continuous space with big tree-like "tubes" that would define the spaces softly instead of relying on traditional hard-edge walls to divide various programs.

I think the concept of "function" seems to be the twentieth-century term that is no longer relevant. I do not have an image of "form" either. I am more interested in creating places similar to the ones found in nature and integrating them within architecture to make people feel like being in nature. I want to remove walls as much as possible to make places connected and free, as if they were in a forest.

Speaking of architecture by Japanese architects of our age I see it merely as the sophistication of modernism. However, the only future of sophistication is further sophistication, and I am not interested in sophistication. My goal is to create modern architecture that has a close relationship with nature.

In conversation with
Toyo Ito, Architect

Zoom video call between
New York, USA and Tokyo, Japan,
June 6, 2021

B. 1941 in Seoul, South Korea;
Lives and practices
in Tokyo, Japan

Close Relationship with
Nature
New Territories—New
Doubts
Expending Modernism
Algorithmic Geometry
Fluid Space

"Architecture Is All About Going with Your Gut"

In conversation with
Helmut Jahn, Architect

Architect's office in Chicago, USA,
August 17, 2018

B. 1940 in Nuremberg, Germany;
Lived and practiced in
Chicago, USA

D. 2021 outside of Chicago, USA

I Just Go Forward;
I Am Fighting
Freedom of Possibilities
Responsive to Structure
Romantic High-Tech
Transparency

The future of your Thompson Center here in Chicago is now uncertain. How do you see its place in history?

When it opened in 1985, it made history because it became a new public place for the city, not just another government building. It was a new way to integrate private space with the public space. Of course, it was never a well-managed public place for political reasons. It is not even open on weekends and there are so many restrictions where people can and can't go. Still, in the future I can imagine it to be used by a private company such as Google. The original idea was to open this building from every side. I started with a solid block. But I felt that the building must have a public plaza, so I cut the corner off on an angle and curved it to represent symbolically a dome of a traditional state capitol. Transparency was the guiding principle. But transparency is not the same as looking straight through a building: it's not just a physical idea, it is also an intellectual one—to read from one layer to the next.

When we enclosed the atrium, I felt that the building lost something. That's why 15 years later, while designing the SONY Center in Berlin the atrium there became the open courtyard. I remember when the chairman of SONY viewed the model and said, "Mr. Jahn, where are the doors?" I said, "There are no doors." And he said, "But then everybody can come in." So, I said, "You got it!" [Laughs.] That's what we tried to do, and he never said anything else.

So, the Thompson Center pushed the SONY Center, which became the new kind of urban space for new society. I look at history both ways—past and future. Look at the public piazza in Siena; that is an inspiration for SONY. One project pushes the next.

Architecture is so difficult. Good architecture is all about going with your gut. You have something on your mind and you just must go ahead and do it.

Portrait: Helmut Jahn (photo © Ingrid von Kruse) **Above:** JAHN, James R. Thompson Center, 17-story all-glass atrium, Chicago, Illinois, USA, 1985 (photo © Rainer Viertlböck)

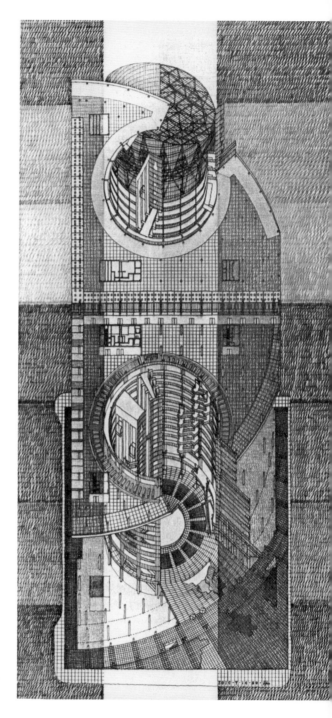

Right and opposite: Helmut Jahn, James R. Thompson Center, Chicago, Illinois, USA, 1985 (drawings courtesy Helmut Jahn)

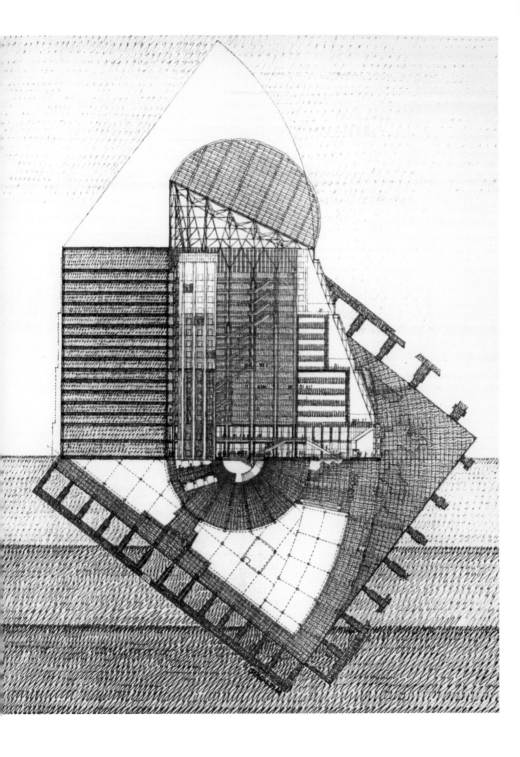

Portrait: Bijoy Jain (photo © Rema Chaudhary) **Above:** Bijoy Jain of Studio Mumbai, MPavilion, Melbourne, Australia, 2016 (photo © John Gollings)

"Architecture Is Not About an Image, It Is About Sensibility"

Regarding your MPavilion design here in Melbourne, you said, "I see it as a place of engagement, a space to discover the essentials of the world and of oneself." What is your architecture about?

For me, architecture is a physical manifestation and precise representation of what it means to be human. It is all about negotiating with the immediate landscape and environment. The act of architecture is about making space, not a building as an object. Yes, it requires a form, but it is more important to discover what each place reverberates.

If we get rid of all the clutter, what fundamentally makes me also fundamentally makes you. We are all connected. We are all driven toward the center manifested in the well of water, which is the essential part of the pavilion. Without the well, it would be just another building floating in the landscape. The well makes it anchored. Architecture is a moment in time, an interface, a communication between ground and sky. When an Aboriginal man prepares to go to sleep, he drives a stick into the ground. The symbolism behind that is to "slow down" the rotation of the Earth, to slow down time during the sleep. I think we all strive for certain lightness, but in recognition that there is weight too. There is a beautiful posture in yoga where half of the body assumes to be rooted into the ground, while the other half strives to go into the sky, like a rocket. The idea of working toward equilibrium is important.

My goal is to be in a situation when things that one can imagine are possible. I don't want to be restricted by building industry or economy. Each problem is mine; each solution is mine. I have a great deal of affection for modernism, but I also want to test and find various ways to connect it to many regional techniques used in India to this day; that is the real focus of my practice. I want to keep searching for what is important here and now. My work is about understanding my own limits and how those limits can be extended. Architecture is not about an image; it is about sensibility.

In conversation with Bijoy Jain of Studio Mumbai, Architect

Architect's hotel in Melbourne, Australia, July 27, 2016

B. 1965 in Mumbai, India; Lives and practices in Mumbai, India

Negotiating Each Moment in Time

Exploring Skills and Materiality

Open, Private, and Intimate

Toward Equilibrium

Toward Lightness

"The Architects' Vocation Is a Futurist Art, Making the World a Better Place"

In conversation
with Charles Jencks,
Architectural Historian
and Landscape Designer

Over the phone between
New York, USA and London, UK,
following multiple face-to-face
meetings, March 28, 2013

B. 1939 in Baltimore, Maryland, USA;
Lived and practiced in London, UK
and Dumfriesshire, Scotland

D. 2019 in London, UK

The Power of Enigma
Iconographic Deficit
Post-Modernism
Iconic Buildings
Pluralist Age

As Oscar Wilde pointed out, "There is only one thing in the world worse than being talked about, and that is not being talked about." Being in the spotlight and getting work are interdependent aspects of our profession, which brings us to the iconic architecture. Is it here to stay despite such strong current resisting forces at play as emphases on sustainability, green principles, social engagement, regionalism, and collaboration?

It was Dinocrates, the Greek architect who anointed his body with oil and draped his left shoulder with a lion's skin to impress the Emperor Alexander the Great, who he then flattered with a design of a mountain in the shape of Alexander holding a city. You can't get more anthropomorphic and literally iconic than that, and this older Western tradition oscillated with periodic bouts of pragmatism and abstraction.

In order to get their firms going, and to get the kind of creatively open projects architects want, they have to play this game, a practical truth. But you should also look at architects as part-time utopians, an idealistic profession since the time of Vitruvius, who believe that they make the society better by pursuing their ideals and serving the public. The architects' vocation is a futurist art, making the world a better place, building for tomorrow. This idealism is manifested in their social works, the "architecture of good intentions" as Colin Rowe called it. But if you don't get the big prestigious jobs, then you can't have the kind of creative freedom liberated by such jobs. That's why all the "usual suspects" must keep competing for iconic projects. Their number will only increase in 10 years, as the concentration of capital tends to produce isolated icons. The same is true in the art world. Personal signature is a strong force, too strong for architects to reverse. We should, of course, resist and bend the forces, as critics and designers, but also debate the iconography, style, metaphors, enigmatic signifiers, and urbanism.

Portrait: Charles Jencks (photo courtesy Charles Jencks) **Above:** Iconic Buildings, collage (image courtesy OMA)

Portrait: Eddie Jones (photo © Paul Markow) **Top:** Jones Studio, Desert Outpost, Private Residence, Paradise Valley, Arizona, USA, 2014 (photo © Bill Timmerman) **Bottom:** Crater House (artist residence), Roden Crater, Coconino County, Arizona, USA, 2017, unbuilt (drawing © Brian Andrews)

"I Hope You Will Never Know What I Am Going to Do Next"

Your buildings have something I have never seen before— eyelashes. I am referring to metal or wood overhangs—some bent into an array of fingers, others straight lines—embellishing views under canopies and out of windows. How did you come up with this eccentric idea?

When Frank Lloyd Wright first arrived in Arizona, he intuitively knew the desert was about dotted lines, as opposed to straight edges. If you look at Taliesin West there is a fascia dentil, as seen in ancient Greek and Roman temples. In most of his Arizona houses you will see a similar dentil making a dotted line. What you refer to as eyelashes, has to do with that idea. My intention was to cast intriguing shadows. I said, "How can I make a fuzzy line?" It was easy! We used a water jet cutter to slice the metal overhang edge in one of my earlier houses, then bent the fingers up and down. Only when we were done, did this detail remind me of eyelashes. Another house, Desert Outpost, is distinguished by randomly cantilevered wood boards to dissipate the edges into air.

Here I must bring up the name of another one of my heroes—Bruce Goff, who influenced my work as much as Wright. I discovered him as a child by stumbling upon his Bavinger House in Norman, Oklahoma, near where my family lived. A fantastic house where everything was suspended off a recycled oil field drill stem, a central mast 55 feet high. My God, there has never been anything like it before or since. Goff never gave up. He was enthusiastic about starting over. If something was too expensive or he missed a certain mark, he would develop a different idea and then, another one. Mies said, "We cannot invent new architecture every Monday morning." But Goff said, "I need to invent new architecture whether it is Monday morning or not." I agree with Goff! You never knew what he was going to do next. And I hope you will never know what I am going to do next. I don't claim that's the way to do architecture. But it's my way and it's a lot of fun!

In conversation with Eddie Jones of Jones Studio, Architect

Skype video call between New York and Tempe, Arizona, USA, September 4, 2020

B. 1949 in Fort Worth, Texas, USA; Lives in Phoenix and practices in Tempe, Arizona, USA

Finding Beauty in Something Ordinary
Child-Like Imagination
Craftsmanship
Refinement
Restraint

"The Closest Image to the Kind of Architecture I Try to Achieve Is a Rainbow"

In conversation with
Kengo Kuma, Architect

Architect's hotel on Columbus
Circle in New York, USA,
November 3, 2008

B. 1954 in Yokohama, Japan;
Lives and practices
in Tokyo, Japan

A Beautiful Shadow Can
Control Everything

Breaking Materials into
Particles

As Weak as a Human Body

Forms Should Be Quiet

Voids

I am fascinated about your idea of erasing architecture by breaking it into particles. Could you go over it?

In traditional Japanese architecture building elements are very small: wood, rice paper, and sometimes stone. Usually there is space in between those elements to allow for natural breezes. I apply these methods in my own architecture in designing modern buildings. I think it is hard to appreciate tactile qualities of materials if they appear as masses. If materials are broken into particles, they become more vivid and transient, like rainbows. At times, they appear as objects, but with the change of light they disperse like clouds and dissolve like mist. To prevent an object from appearing, that is to erase architecture. My aim is not to create particle-like works of architecture. I want to create a condition as vague and ambiguous as drifting particles. The closest image to the kind of architecture I try to achieve is a rainbow. We must reverse our form of perception. Instead of looking at architecture from the outside, we must look at the environment from within.

I think of materials as basic ingredients for making things. Materials can't be too big or too small. If the particles are too large, they become like a mass. If they are too fine—they may also appear like a mass. Their size must be determined in response to the distance between them and the observer, the relative size of other particles and the framing. In the design of Bato Hiroshige Museum of Art, I spaced louvers vertically for the first time. I was inspired by Ando Hiroshige's beautiful painting *People on a Bridge Surprised by Rain*. Selecting particles, their size and details, is the central focus of my architecture.

Portrait: Kengo Kuma (photo © James Gibbs) **Above:** Kengo Kuma & Associates,
Bato Hiroshige Museum of Art, Tochigi, Japan, 2000 (photo © Mitsumasa Fujitsuka)

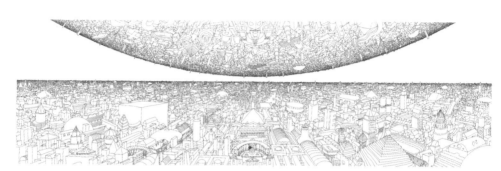

Portrait: Totan Kuzembaev (photo courtesy Totan Kuzembaev) Top: City Sphere-Cube (drawing © Totan Kuzembaev)
Bottom: Totan Kuzembaev, Architect's House, Kaluga, Russia, 2020 (photo courtesy Totan Kusembaev)

"A House Needs to Grow Like a Child, a Flower, or a Tree"

You once said, "If you want to puzzle an architect let him be free. If I were told—do as you please, I wouldn't know where to begin. There would be no starting point. There would be nothing for me to fight with." If architecture is a fight, what are you fighting with or whom?

The most interesting architecture happens when the architect finds an unexpected solution in a desperate situation. That's how I see the architect's role. But if you need to place a house in an open field with no restrictions, I don't believe anything interesting will come out of that. Architecture is a reaction to a challenge, client's request, or particularity of the site. Any condition is an advice to the architect, a guidance of sort. Personally, I feel lost without it because otherwise you can do just about anything. I need to examine the site, see where the sun rises, identify the views, understand the topography. I want to know why the client has purchased the site. I am also informed by the material, budget. An architect can't be a pure artist. I can't even imagine a situation when I would sit down and come up with a house detached from its place. A house can't be pretentious. The vision comes by itself, subconsciously, while responding to such details as trying to save a tree or rising high enough to clear a particular view. A house needs to grow like a child, like a flower, or a tree. There is no preconceived image. Instead, it is about following a path—from one challenge to the next, responding to the architect's imagination. As an architect, I depend on my clients' ambitions and I get so much pleasure out of that. [Laughs.]

Architecture is like a person—it gets born and then it dies. In other words, once a house has lived its life it needs to die. Another person will come to build a new house. I am against preservation. Many of my houses are built out of wood and they change all the time, and quite naturally. This is wonderful—a person is changing, and his house is changing with him. The person is getting wise and the house is getting wise as well.

In conversation with
Totan Kuzembaev, Architect

WhatsApp video call between New York, USA and Moscow, Russia, January 8, 2021

B. 1953 in Aryss district of Chekment region of Kazakhstan; Lives and practices in Moscow, Russia

Exposed Structure Is Architecture's Embellishment
Following a Path—From One Challenge to the Next
Aiming at Achieving Simplicity
Never-Ending Improvisation
Guided by Restrictions

"The Intention Is to Provoke More Awareness and Inquiries"

In conversation with Nic Lehoux, Photographer

Samuel Paley Park, East 53rd Street in Manhattan, New York, USA, May 11, 2012

B. 1968 in Quebec City, Canada; Lives in the Pacific Northwest, USA; works around the world

A Decisive Moment
Theater of Life
Perseverance
I Take Risks
Evolution

Your images appear to be effortless. How laborious are they in reality?

A lot of work goes into preparation of every shot or composition. For example, when I photographed Renzo Piano's New York Times Building at night a lot of coordination had to be done to make sure the lighting was on throughout the building. I had assistants and architects running around on all floors to make sure the motion-controlled lights stayed on. And I had to bribe the security guards at the adjacent building with a case of beer to get access to the perfect roof level to take the shot. It was my job to shoot the best possible and evocative images. In order to take the picture I want, I find it sometimes necessary to hang off buildings. The key is to create your own identity and signature. I take risks. I have used my rock-climbing experience to get a picture I want.

What I am hoping is for the viewer to ask the question— wow, how could this happen? The intention is to provoke more awareness and inquiries. How viable is the world and societal fabric that we are building? How environmentally conscious are we by going through so many cycles of construction and destruction? Artistically, I am looking for beauty. For me beauty is a sense of purity and honesty of the moment when there is no anticipation of something or preconceived notion of what is about to happen, when things are not arranged or designed, but instead just happen. Rough nature is beautiful. People on the street, in the farmers markets, on the beach ... The theater of life that surrounds us all the time—the collision of people within the environment we live in, their spontaneous interaction with each other—that is beauty! Fleeting moments that will never happen again. Beauty to me is a very remote idea from the kind of plastic beauty that so often surrounds us in modern life.

Portrait: Nic Lehoux (photo © Denis Schofield) **Above:** Yujiapu New City Under Construction, the Binhai New Area of Tianjin, China, 2017 (photo © Nic Lehoux) **Left:** OMA, Pierre Lassonde Pavilion, Musée National des Beaux-Arts du Québec, Quebec City, Canada, 2016 (photo © Nic Lehoux) **Following pages:** Renzo Piano Building Workshop, New York Times Building, New York, USA, 2007 (photo © Nic Lehoux)

155

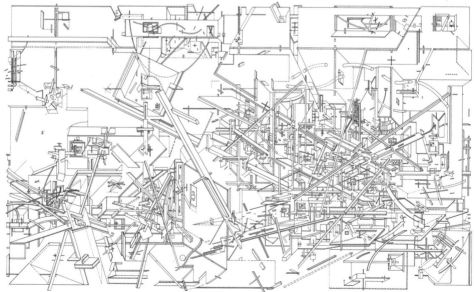

Portrait: Daniel Libeskind (photo © Stefan Ruiz) Top: Studio Libeskind, Denver Art Museum, Denver, Colorado, USA, 2006 (photo © Alex Fradkin) Bottom: *Micromegas*, Drawing Series, 1979 (drawing © Studio Libeskind)

"You Have to Follow the Signs That Are Meant Only for You"

Could you talk about your early projects, the Micromegas *and* Chamberworks *drawing series? You seem to go back to these sorts of architectural meditations, as if they were telling you what to do next. They make up your work's DNA. Would you agree?*

Well, a meditation is a passive term, but these drawings are really transformations of the world the way we know it. They have a quality of detachment from an immediate task, but they are also a source for transformations. They are drifting in no-man's-land between reality and dreams, the world of the unknown. I don't look at them as if they were a crystal ball to figure out a new plan. But the drawings themselves speak up. They are, in a way, instruments for architectural thinking. They unravel, project, and show new directions. My projects are about gathering traces; traces of statistics, symbols, narratives, legends, dreams, myths ...

I think with every project you have to start with a new wonder and new encounters, but it is never a tabula rasa. Architecture is not just about materials. It is about an idea, spirit, and culture. And that is an ongoing quest, which is reflected in drawings, writings, and buildings. Architecture is a world. It is not a building. Every building, every city should have a story—a story about people. If there is no story then it is just a hunk of metal, glass, and concrete, nothing else. There is no future there. Otherwise, a building is an object, an abstraction. Architecture is very crucial to understanding many things because it provides space to see the sky, to see the street, to see others as they enter through the door. I like following many paths. I never set myself a goal. The goal is unknown. My goal is to stay on the path of exploring architecture. You have to follow the signs that are meant only for you. I lean toward forms that lead to a point and that try to make a point.

In conversation with
Daniel Libeskind of
Studio Libeskind, Architect

Architect's office in New York, USA, August 31, 2011

B. 1946 in Łódź, Poland; Lives and practices in New York, USA

Instruments for
Thinking and
Unraveling
Who Are We? Where
Are We Going?
Dreams, Memories, and
Stories
Language of
Communication
Something Radical

"The Container Is a Vehicle to Invent New Architecture"

In conversation with Ada Tolla and Giuseppe Lignano of LOT-EK, Architects

Your work is about rethinking the box, the shipping container. Why do you go back to it again and again and how does it help you to enrich your architecture?

Architects' studio in New York, USA, October 26, 2017

Ada Tolla: B. 1964 in Potenza, Italy; Lives, practices, and teaches in New York, USA

Giuseppe Lignano: B. 1963 in Naples, Italy; Lives, practices, and teaches in New York, USA

Chance, Intention, Assembly

Super-Rational and Playful

Permanent—Temporary

Raw and Conceptual

Stationary—Mobile

AT: There are materials and objects that we are interested in, the shipping container is one of them. To us, it is an ongoing speculation. From the beginning our work has been about responding to things we found around us, on the streets of New York—a piece of furniture, a cardboard box, packaging foam—and questioning what we could do with them; in the spirit of true gleaners, or "upcyclers," before the word was even invented. We like assembling and disassembling, reinventing space, reimagining uses. One day we entered a whole depot of shipping containers in New Jersey. We realized immediately the potential of this box and began altering this at once dumb and intelligent object, able to be picked up, moved from ship to train to truck, and capable of global reach. Our intention is to engage with leftovers and overproduction, and to do it with a positive attitude. We are curious about cutting these things into pieces and slices. We are interested in these discoveries and provocations. We are excited to radically transform the ordinary. Over, and over, and over. There is always another possibility.

GL: First, we are architects, and we wish that our work would be seen independently of the fact that we use containers. It is not just about the containers; it is about what can be done with them. For us, the container is a vehicle to invent new architecture. We use even conventional materials very unconventionally. We often expose things that are typically buried behind walls. We always try to find our own way of seeing and using things. Discipline is the key. Our work is more conceptual than compositional. The idea of creating new spaces and new aesthetics is important to us. On the one hand, we want our architecture to be low-tech, handmade, textured, brutal, organic, and romantic. On the other hand, we want it to be high-tech, geometric, graphic, abstract, perfect, and otherworldly, like a dream. We want to create tension and balance between these extreme ideas. We design our projects by making and building things, not by drawing something from scratch.

Portrait: Ada Tolla and Giuseppe Lignano (photo © Aundre Larrow) **Above:** LOT-EK,
Residential loft with petroleum trailer tank repurposed into two sleeping pods,
West Village, New York, USA, 2000 (photo © Paul Warchol)

Portrait: Petra Bachmaier and Sean Gallero (photo © Nathan Keay) **Above:** Luftwerk in collaboration with Iker Gil, *Geometry of Light*, German Pavilion, Barcelona, Spain, 2019 (photo © Kate Joyce)

"A Combination of Light and Color Can Be Magical"

You define yourselves as light artists. What are the roles of light and architecture in your art?

SG: People sometimes confuse us with lighting designers, but we are definitely artists! Lighting designers achieve the right ambiance. We work on creating a particular revelation and experience. We work with narratives. First and foremost, we are installation artists. Our work resides in the intersection of design, art, and architecture. We are inspired by natural light. We are intrigued by such conditions as light coming through trees in a forest or reflected in moving water. We are inspired by such incidental beautiful qualities that we try to imitate, and we use technology to stimulate organic, natural feelings. Light helps to reveal things. Light gives objects, buildings, and surfaces a different quality. For example, when buildings are illuminated in a particular way they are perceived and felt differently. At night they become completely different creatures. We enjoy playing with materiality of buildings.

PB: The idea is to reveal surfaces and textures; to reveal a particular history, a story, or to bring light into a moment. The point is to make you look at things in a new way; to capture a particular quality of light or what it illuminates. How do you shape this magical phenomenon of light? Light can be shaped and sculpted, and we want to play with it to create new settings and experiences in a variety of ways. Light is an inexhaustible source of inspiration. It allows to make so many discoveries. We look a lot at the quality of light and how it illuminates surfaces and spaces. We also like exploring colors. A combination of light and color can be magical.

In conversation with
Petra Bachmaier and Sean Gallero
of Luftwerk, Light Artists

Zoom video call between
New York and Chicago, USA,
February 14, 2020

Petra Bachmaier: B. 1974 in
Munich, Germany; Lives and
practices in Chicago, USA

Sean Gallero: B. 1973 in The Bronx,
New York, USA; Lives and
practices in Chicago, USA

Shift and Alter People's
Perception
Revealing Geometry
of Light
The Idea of Sculpting
Light
Architecture Is a Canvas
Light and Color

"People May Say My Work Is Futuristic, But I See It as Traditional"

In conversation with Ma Yansong of MAD Architects, Architect

MAD Architects' office in Beijing, China, March 27, 2017

B. 1975 in Beijing, China; Lives and practices in Beijing, China

Creating Illusions and Atmospheres

Emotional Connection to Nature

Newly Imagined Spaces

I Am Curious

Undefined

You said, "I think it is important to practice architecture with an attitude." What does it mean to you—to practice architecture with an attitude?

It means being critical about the context and thinking about what kind of cultural impact we want to leave in our urban centers. Here is my attitude—I close my eyes, I close my ears, and I don't want to communicate with the manmade world; I only want to relate to the nature in front of me. I bring the idea of *Shan Shui*, traditional Chinese brush and ink landscape paintings, into my architecture. *Shan Shui* is a philosophy; it is about establishing an emotional connection to nature. If you insert our buildings into a traditional Chinese landscape painting, they will fit just right. But if you look around and compare them to other buildings, you may see them as something very bold and conflicting. I am looking for ways to adapt Chinese traditions of blending nature and architecture to contemporary architecture on an urban scale. And I want everything to look new and different every time. Architecture should be constantly evolving. There are so many ways to look at things, which means there is no reality, in a way. All reality is an illusion. I want to discover my own reasons for everything. Your own reaction and your own feelings should be what you believe in. As an architect, I am not creating realities or facts with my objects. I am creating illusions and atmospheres. Here is what I want—to bring something unfamiliar into my projects. I want to build buildings that no one has ever seen before. People may see my work as futuristic, but I see it as traditional because I carry old Eastern philosophy and use it to respond to new challenges. To me architecture is a conversation, in which I look back to the past and project my ideas into the future. Architecture is art, attitude, and emotions, all interlinked.

Portrait: Ma Yansong (photo courtesy MAD Architects) Top: MAD Architects, Harbin
Opera House, Harbin, China, 2015 (photo © Adam Mork) Bottom: MAD Architects,
YueCheng Courtyard Kindergarten, Beijing, China, 2020 (photo © Hufton+Crow)

Portrait: Fumihiko Maki (photo © Richard Schulman) **Above:** Maki and Associates,
Spiral Building, Tokyo, Japan, 1985 (photo © Toshiharu Kitajima)

"We All Wanted to Be Ourselves"

Years ago, you said, "I have no inspiration, just hard work." You also said, "Architecture is not about invention, but about discovery." Could you elaborate?

I think architecture is not like art. It must be used. So, if anything, it is a kind of social art. For me architecture is an endless process for learning. I observe how people use our buildings and I try to incorporate those findings in the next project. So, my architecture is done through accumulation of knowledge and experience of designing and building for many decades now. Testing ideas is important.

I worked with Kenzo Tange and I learned from him simply by observing his design process. His architecture was his own and none of the architects who worked for him— [Arata] Isozaki, [Kisho] Kurokawa, [Yoshio] Taniguchi, and I, as well as many others—tried to imitate his work. We all wanted to be ourselves. We respected him, but we wanted to be different. Of course, there are architects who choose to imitate their masters, such as in the case of the many followers of Wright, Mies, or Le Corbusier. Perhaps that was Tange's lesson—the process itself was important, but there should be many ways to express architecture.

As you know, I was one of the founding members of the Metabolist movement with Isozaki, Kurokawa, and [Kiyonori] Kikutake. The reason it did not last was because we each had different ideas, becoming busy with individual projects. We went our own ways. I was predominantly interested in high-density living. I think we realized early on that cities need to evolve over time, not be planned in a forced way. So, we decided not to interfere. All collaborative efforts come to an end, eventually, as was in the case of Archigram and Team X. And individually, we all had very different ideas about the future of cities.

In conversation with
Fumihiko Maki, Architect

Architect's office Maki and Associates in Tokyo, Japan, March 12, 2018

B. 1928 in Tokyo, Japan; Lives and practices in Tokyo, Japan

Respect Human Behavior
Time—Space—Existence
Minimalist Approach
High-Density Living
Exposed Concrete

"I Want Architecture Itself to Lead Us to Potential Discoveries"

In conversation with Jürgen Mayer H. of J. MAYER H. und Partner, Architekten, Architect

Architect's office in Berlin, Germany, July 17, 2018

B. 1965 in Stuttgart, Germany; Lives and practices in Berlin, Germany

Communication and Collaboration

Transferability and Economy

Critique and Discourse

Identities and Options

Patterns

Your work is inspired by data protection patterns. How did this fascination begin and how do you translate these patterns into architecture?

It all started around 1995, when I presented *Housewarming* at Randolph Street Gallery in Chicago, an installation with temperature-sensitive materials. There were surfaces painted with a thermochromic carbon-based pigment that fades as the temperature rises and brightens as it cools. The idea was about making visible what is typically not visible and exposing private information to the public. While working on this exhibit, I discovered that data protection patterns could be used as metaphors in architecture in such border situations that deal with something private behind and public in front, or neutral versus personalized. I used these patterns with a special temperature-sensitive ink silkscreened on paper to create the show's guest book—people would write in it and not see the writing, but once they pressed on the writing with warm hands the pattern disappeared to reveal the text.

Patterns come in all kinds of variations: numbers, letters, graphics, cross hatchings, company logos, and so on. Data protection patterns have become our main source of inspiration. The more we work with them the more elaborate our surfaces and spaces become. We use these patterns in all possible scales and projects—from art installations to urban complexes. These patterns envelope and contain spaces and highlight ambivalent border situations between inside and outside. Every time, the design process varies. Sometimes we may get inspired by a fragment of a particular pattern and it may be used very directly as an element in our project. For us, patterns are metaphors that inspire us to do something that is not always visible at first. I see our projects as lenses, through which the surrounding context is looked at to see something new. I am searching for architecture that would foresee changes, or better yet, allow inventive social changes to take place. I want architecture itself to lead us to potential discoveries.

Portrait: Jürgen Mayer H. (photo © Jens Passoth) **Above:** J. MAYER H., *RAPPORT*, exhibition, Berlinische Galerie, Berlin, Germany, 2011–12 (photo © Ludger Paffrath)

Portrait: Thom Mayne (photo © Richard Schulman) **Top:** Morphosis, Cooper Union for the Advancement of Science and Art, New York, USA, 2006 (photo © Alex Fradkin) **Bottom left & right:** Morphosis, Caltrans District 7 Headquarters, Los Angeles, USA, 2004 (photos © Nic Lehoux)

"Look, This Is What You Are Capable of If You Just Let Your Mind Free!"

In your mind, your architecture is natural and consequential. Yet, your work projects very different notions. You describe it with the following words: partial completion, typological hybrid, a language of assemblage and idiosyncrasies, spatial variation, tension, resistance, and confrontation. Why do you want your architecture to embrace these notions? Where does this idea of challenging the norm come from?

From birth. From my DNA! One kid is looking outside of a window and the world is just OK, and he can fit in and do well. And another kid looks outside of the same window and it makes no sense to him at all. It is as simple as that. We are all different but what we do seems normal to us, no matter what we do. The difference between architects lies in what kind of questions they are asking or not asking. We live in a vastly pluralistic world.

I am an architect and I am interested in making exciting buildings. I love architecture that starts with impossibilities. I love the complexities, in which architecture is embedded. I am interested in anything and everything that potentially may affect our work. And I have no interest in any particular trajectory. I have no idea where I am going. I live totally in the present and I deal with questions in front of me. Anything can become an inspiration. I am a pragmatic idealist. Today, the issue I am interested most about is urbanization, which in the twenty-first century will supersede individual buildings. What is missing today is the collective discourse; instead, so much energy is spent on criticizing the individual. But I love extravagant buildings such as Louis Vuitton Foundation in Paris by [Frank] Gehry. This project is powered by such exceptional imagination. This building is done by a Miles Davis of contemporary architecture, showing the absolute maximum of capability of our discipline. This is a kind of building that you would take a kid to and say, "Look, this is what you are capable of if you just let your mind free!"

In conversation with
Thom Mayne of Morphosis,
Architect

Architect's office in New York,
USA, May 5, 2016

B. 1944 in Waterbury, Connecticut,
USA; Lives, practices, and teaches
in Los Angeles and New York, USA

Misalignments and
Complexities
Apparent
Contradictions
Notion of Randomness
Multiplicity of Forces
Pursuit of Ambiguity

"We, Architects, Think of Ourselves as Politicians"

In conversation with Giancarlo
Mazzanti of EL EQUIPO
MAZZANTI, Architect

Architect's hotel near
Columbus Circle, Manhattan,
New York, USA, November 18, 2011

B. 1963 in Barranquilla, Colombia;
Lives and practices in Bogotá,
Colombia; teaches in USA

Building in
Disadvantaged Parts of
Cities

Operations and Social
Actions

Identities to
Communities

Social Transformer

Transform Mindset

Let's dream a little. If you were the next mayor of Bogotá what project would you work on realizing first?

I would realize two projects. One would connect our city parks to the surrounding mountains, which are beautiful and not used as part of the city. And the second project would be a series of small interactive spaces and installations in poor parts of the city, which should encourage curiosity. They could also be used by local musical bands to add to the identity of various neighborhoods.

I think now is the time to think of how architecture can change the city and the world. Architects can assume that role and make a real difference in how people live and behave. In Colombia, architecture is politics and we, architects, think of ourselves as politicians. We work very closely with our local governments on coming up with strategies for improving communities. Previous generations of architects thought of how architecture could interpret the world, but now is the time to think of how architecture can change the world. We can achieve this by introducing new possibilities for communal interaction. Forms alone can't change anything. People need to be engaged with one another. A good example is the work of Cedric Price whose projects, such as Fun Palace, advocated the role of architecture for nurturing social development by being flexible, indeterminate, and open-ended. In our own architecture, we try to offer opportunities for interactive learning and leisure. For example, not only am I designing educational spaces, where a class takes place, but insert interesting spaces in between where students can interact, or local community meetings can occur. Space itself can be pedagogical by introducing different materials, colors, and creating new identities and provoking interests. I am interested in architecture that encourages people to wonder and to act.

Portrait: Giancarlo Mazzanti (photo © Juan Pablo Salgado) **Above:** EL EQUIPO MAZZANTI,
El Porvenir Social Kindergarten, Bogotá, Colombia, 2009 (photo © Rodrigo Dávila)

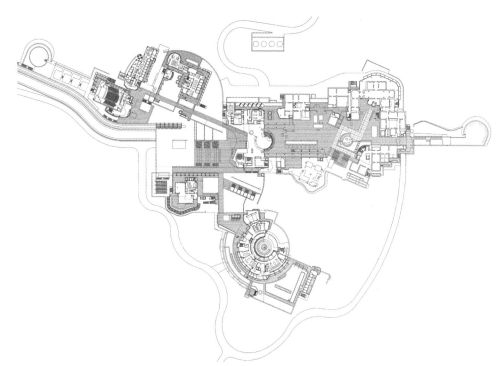

"Whiteness Is What Distinguishes Manmade from Natural"

The Getty Center is the most prominent of your projects. There were over one hundred restrictions in the guidelines, including not to use the color white. But what wasn't compromised was your idea of the grid. Could you explain?

It is true, the entire Getty Center is laid out on a 30-by-30-inch grid. And it works horizontally, as well as vertically, which is very hard to do. All my projects are laid on grids, but the grid usually varies, depending on a situation and what seems appropriate. I always try to have a module. Sometimes we start with one dimension and end up with a very different one for many different reasons. Remember that a module is not something rigid that you can't change within a system. You can have the same distance between the columns and a variety of additional modular systems.

Unfortunately, we could not use white there. First, white articulates the volume—it articulates architectural ideas in the clearest way. The linear elements such as window frames or handrails juxtaposed against plainer elements read most clearly in white. Second, white buildings always change color, and diverse colors of nature are always reflected and refracted in the whiteness of a white building. To me, that's very important. White has many colors. In my first projects, I used painted wood, and then, I discovered metal panels, a durable material that could last and that could express ideas inherent in my architecture. Metal panels, of course, could be used not only in rectilinear forms, but also in curves and fluid shapes that one couldn't do with other materials.

My preference for using white color began with reading about the work of Frank Lloyd Wright. He talked about organic and natural materials and the fact that architecture was organic. But architecture is not organic. You cut down a tree, and it is no longer organic or living; it is static. When you use the wood, you must protect it. Either you seal it, or you paint it. Painting the wood is what preserves it. So, the whiteness is what distinguishes manmade from natural.

In conversation with
Richard Meier, Architect

Architect's office in New York, USA, October 20, 2003

B. 1934 in Newark, New Jersey, USA; Lives and practices in New York, USA

Filled with Light
Transparent
Rational
White
Open

"Architecture Does Not Desire to Be Functional; It Wants to Be Opportune"

In conversation with Paulo Mendes da Rocha, Architect

Architect's office in São Paulo, Brazil, April 7, 2014

B. 1928 in Vitória, Brazil; Lived and practiced in São Paulo, Brazil

D. 2021 in São Paulo, Brazil

Knowledge and Skills
A Symbolic Gesture
Methodology
Confidence
Discourse

You are unquestionably the leading architect in Brazil today. Yet, as you told me there is a law here that does not allow teaching after the age of 70. It is a pity that the wisest can't teach. Can you tell me about your work?

I used to teach the final year of the design studio. I would not try to influence the students too much because they were almost professional architects themselves. Of course, they think they know everything; the reality is that no one knows anything. But a good teacher must act like he knows. Confidence is very important, not only knowledge. Every problem requires thinking, not readymade solutions. You know that you don't know, but there is urgency to do something. You have to discover the knowledge—that's the whole point. I think it is not possible to teach architecture. Every project is an emergency. You must go there and see what needs to be done. You can only teach architects to think by empowering them with knowledge and skills. If you don't know how to read or write you can't come up with a poem. It is all about extracting knowledge from such disciplines as anthropology, geology, structural mechanics, building construction, design, and so on to come up with a spatial interpretation, which is called architecture. I don't search for new shapes; I search for results that work.

Some architects are true artists. Oscar Niemeyer was a very close friend and I admire what he did. He was like Picasso, a great artist. You can't put him into any category. He was unique. No one knows how to read architecture. [Laughs.] It is like literature—the author writes for everyone, but it is for people to interpret the meanings. Architecture could be anything and its interpretations are limitless. Architecture does not desire to be functional; it wants to be opportune.

176

Portrait: Paulo Mendes da Rocha (photo © Andrea Altemulher) **Above:** Paulo Mendes da Rocha, Gymnasium in the Paulistano Athletics Club (architect's first major project), São Paulo, Brazil, 1957 (photo © José Moscardi)

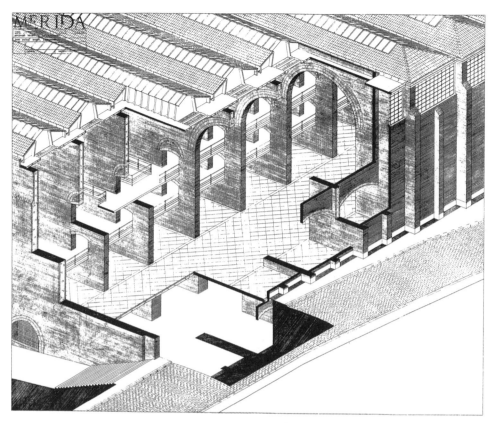

Portrait: Rafael Moneo (photo © Massimiliano Polles)
Above: National Museum of Roman Art in Merida,
Spain, 1980–86 (hand drawing courtesy Rafael Moneo)
Right: Rafael Moneo, National Museum of Roman Art
in Merida, Spain, 1980–86 (photo © Michael Moran for
Rafael Moneo) Following pages: Rafael Moneo, Murcia
City Hall, Murcia, Spain, 1991–98 (photo © Michael Moran
for Rafael Moneo)

"I Don't Have a Fear of Not Having a Common Language"

From early on, parallel to practicing you were very active in writing about architecture. What was it that you wanted to address in your writings?

For me to be critical it helps to find the way to explain what you do as an architect. Extending this approach, I like to establish a dialogue with my colleagues' work. Writing is the way for me to understand architects' works and intentions. I like to explain projects by discovering ideas and identifying problems. Architecture is important as a part of history, but also as a critical discipline. Architecture schools must pay close attention to the contemporary scene. I would like to keep a critical and reflective mind.

Practicing architecture is about adjusting a particular building type to the site. I never dismiss context, but I would argue that my work is not simply contextual. I am always looking beyond context. I am curious. I am working against and with the context—adjusting a building's volume to specific site particularities, looking for what the site needs and what the building wants to become by playing with rhythms, proportions, spacing between various elements, emphasizing clarity of construction means. Good architecture is able to absorb the context and become something else—innovative but rooted in its place. I see cities as layers of materiality. Most of my projects are additions, not new visions from the ground up. I find it very satisfying in taking part in major projects that work in favor of the city—growing, adapting, and making it healthier for people to live and enjoy. This is what I mean when I say that I would like history to be alive.

Most importantly, you can never simply rely on your knowledge. That's not enough. You must keep learning all the time, you have to keep accumulating knowledge by traveling, visiting projects, reading history and criticism, exchanging ideas with colleagues and students. You have to be intuitive, creative, and you must question what you already know all the time. That's why I never tried to develop a singular mode or a style. I always expanded and used a mixture of strategies. I don't have a fear of not having a common language.

In conversation with
Rafael Moneo, Architect

Architect's studio in Madrid, Spain, November 27, 2019

B. 1937 in Tudela, Spain; Lives, practices, and teaches in Madrid, Spain

Looking Beyond Context
Without Compromise
Courage and Attitude
Contemporaneity
A Part of History

"Rather than Working with Forms, We Work with Forces"

In conversation with
Toshiko Mori, Architect

Architect's studio in New York, USA, April 11, 2016

B. 1951 in Kobe, Japan; Lives, practices, and teaches in New York and Boston, USA

Multitasking and Loose Fit

Dialogue and Imagination

Listening and Observing

Strategy of Contrast

Fictional Narrative

You are playing with different ways of how to position and hold buildings. Could you touch on your ways of shaping and placing them?

That's right. As architects, we always fight against gravity. To pretend that gravity doesn't exist is not honest. But we can play with this fundamental fact by creating an illusion of winning over it in various ways. Sure, rather than working with forms, we work with forces. And we work collaboratively with engineers from the very beginning. The house in Ghent, in New York State, which is broken down into several pavilions, presented many such challenges. Not only did we have to resolve each volume structurally and spatially, but also how to pin these pavilions to the rocks where they are sited and make them appear to be floating by hiding the structure underneath. But not directly below, so you can't see the structure. The Thread Cultural Center in Senegal is very different. It is designed parametrically because we tried to come up with the most effective use of structure and local materials, such as bamboo, mud brick, and thatch. Also, the idea was to have a building that would have a roof with a maximum surface to provide deep shade and collect the maximum amount of rainwater. We also needed to catch as much wind as possible to have a constant breeze under the roof. And we wanted to work with what they had and to employ local laborers, not simply bring something already prebuilt. So, the building's form was the result of all these factors, not the other way around. And, of course, the design was influenced by vernacular cylindrical houses they have in the area. You can say that in this project elements of observation were stronger than elements of pure imagination. The main goal was—the residents had to accept this building as their own, and not as a foreign object.

Portrait: Toshiko Mori (photo © Ralph Gibson) **Above:** Toshiko Mori, Thread Artists' Residences & Cultural Center, Sinthian, Senegal, 2015 (photo © Iwan Baan)

Portrait: Eric Owen Moss (photo courtesy Eric Owen Moss Architects) **Top & bottom left:** Eric Owen Moss Architects, Samitaur, Culver City, Los Angeles, USA, 1996 (photo © Tom Bonner) **Bottom right:** Eric Owen Moss Architects, National Conference Room, Culver City, Los Angeles, USA, 1988 (photo © Tom Bonner) **Following pages:** *My List* (little sketch models), ongoing (image courtesy Eric Owen Moss Architects)

"The Truth Is in the Tension of Possibilities"

Your way of making architecture is about being inquisitive and searching for something new—uncovering new ways of imagining architecture. What is the origin of this approach and what is your ultimate goal?

If you are a writer you know what a sentence is—it starts with a capital letter, there should be a noun, a verb, and it should end with a period. That's not how architecture works. I want to say something or at least to have a discussion, or to share my own hypothesis. I may not even be right, but maybe I am. I think we need this tension. The truth is in the tension of possibilities. What's important is to be investigative. That's what to me means to be alive as an architect. It is a way of life. It has nothing to do with whether there is a consensus or agreement. The idea is for me not to allow becoming a rule or a system. I am against becoming predictable. The question for me is this—can I free myself from being conservative, predictable, and conventional?

My dad was a writer and when he wasn't writing he was making his lists of words—rhymes, synonyms, antonyms, and so on to stretch the vocabulary. That's what I learned from him. So, now I have my own list—little sketch models. I keep making them almost every day. They are different from one another or they can be similar, or contradictory to one another. They have no site, no budget, no program, no owner, no zoning restrictions. They are these little dances of forms and shapes, and spaces, ideas, or pieces of ideas. They help me to keep my thinking going. They are my instincts, my inquiries. They distract me. They inform me. The idea is to stretch the reality of possibilities. It gives me something to start. Ultimately, it is about the learning process, which evolves.

In conversation with
Eric Owen Moss, Architect

Skype video call between
New York and Los Angeles, USA,
May 22, 2020

B. 1943 in Los Angeles, California, USA; Lives, practices, and teaches in Los Angeles, California, USA

Uncertainty and
Resistance
Questioning
Conventions
Skeptical and
Suspicious
Making and Unmaking
Unlearning

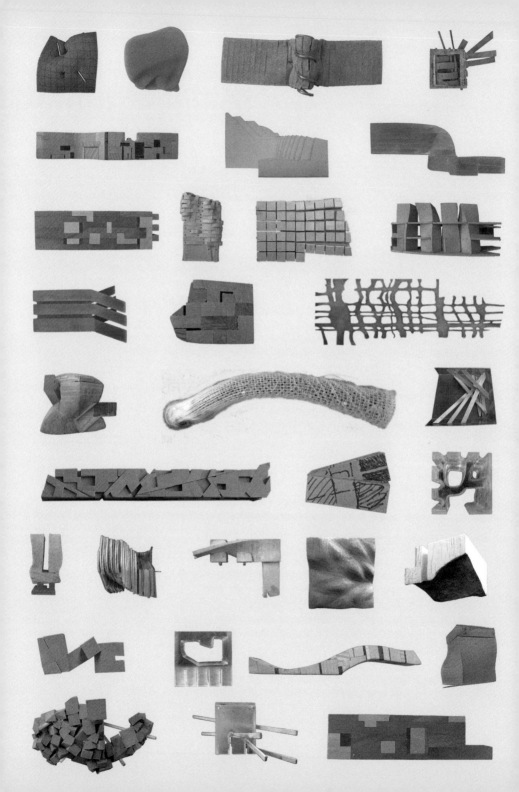

"Any Work of Architecture That Exists or Has a Potential to Exist Is There to Be Discovered"

In conversation with
Glenn Murcutt, Architect

Architect's home in Mosman,
near Sydney, Australia,
September 3, 2013

B. 1936 in London, UK; Lives
and practices in Mosman, near
Sydney; teaches in Australia

Responsive and
Responsible
Vernacular Architecture
Clarity and Simplicity
Ordinary Attitude
Rain Falling

You said, "Works of architecture are discovered, not designed." In other words, your houses respond to climatic conditions; they are described as "instruments" or "devices with which to sense nature." What are the inspirations that help you in your process of discovering architecture?

Any work of architecture that exists or has a potential to exist is there to be discovered. I am not creating anything. My role is to discover—just like Michelangelo would say: "Every block of stone has a statue inside it, and it is the task of the sculptor to discover it." I think there is a problem with the idea of creating things. There is arrogance in it. There is a creative process on the path to discovery. I don't need a manifesto. I have a very ordinary attitude in life, which is to do ordinary things extraordinarily well.

My inspirations are music, light, fauna, flora. I research the social history, ancient history, modern history; look at the geology, hydrology, geomorphology, water levels, nutrients, why certain trees grow in particular areas. I look at the climate throughout the year, sun position, humidity, rainfall, wind patterns ... I collect all this data. That's why just like trees are different, depending on where they grow, the projects are also very different based on all these factors.

There are so many buildings that exclude nature. But I want to smell the rain, hear the rain falling ... I am collecting water—nature's gift, to be reused and to be returned to the land again. To do that one must design a building so nature is the musical score, the occupants are the audience, and the building is the instrument, through which it is allowed all these things to take place. The insulation used on the roof can give you a particular sound of the water falling ... The way I design windows, they can be opened even when the rain is very heavy—to look at the water coming over the sheet of glass and all the beautiful patterns ... Imagine—sitting at the veranda, and seeing the water coming down in layers—how beautiful is that! The most important thing to me is the junction of the rational and the poetic.

Portrait: Glenn Murcutt (photo by Anthony Browell, courtesy Architecture Foundation Australia)
Above: Glenn Murcutt, Magney House, Bingie Point, New South Wales, Australia, 1982–84, 1999
(photo by Anthony Browell, courtesy Architecture Foundation Australia)

Portrait: Lyndon Neri and Rossana Hu (photo © Jiaxi Yang and Zhu Zhe) Above: Neri&Hu, The Commune Social Restaurant, Shanghai, China, 2013 (photo © Pedro Pegenaute)

"We Believe in the Poetic over the Utilitarian"

How would you define your architecture's identity?

RH: We believe in architecture and design as a powerful cultural force. Designers use theory as a crutch; they find reasons or famous quotes to support their choices. And there are examples of certain projects that if you don't know about the theory or history behind them then they may not be perceived as beautiful. Projects are accompanied by stories that help a lot. If the story is not told, the meaning and appreciation may be lost. There must be a clear idea and if it resonates, then details may vary. Apart from beauty we operate with ideas that are metaphoric, poetic, and nostalgic by referencing the past to move toward the future. We are looking for the poetic. We believe in the subtext over the obvious and the poetic over the utilitarian. There is a need for abstraction, to express the meaning without being obvious and literal. So, if we can bring poetry through space, light, form, and materials to a person who comes to our building then we will be happy.

LN: We deal with a number of obsessions. In the first few years, it was more about personal obsessions and lately, we are more interested in community-based obsessions. One of our obsessions is the notion of nostalgia. The fact that we both came out of the Chinese diaspora has a lot to do with it. We had been unearthing this idea until we came across what is called "reflective nostalgia," a concept articulated by the late Russian-American Harvard professor and novelist Svetlana Boym. In the context of the rapid growth of China's economy it resonated with us and since then it has become one of our guiding principles. We treat historical buildings as urban artifacts and for us they are never just about the past. Another obsession for our work deals with what we call total design, the idea of being able to see each project from the point of view of different disciplines and perspectives. Apart from architecture we get involved in doing interiors, furniture design, product design, and graphics. We find different ways of analyzing projects and solving problems.

In conversation with Lyndon Neri and Rossana Hu of Neri&Hu, Architects

Neri&Hu office in Shanghai, China, March 11, 2019

Lyndon Neri: B. 1965 in The Philippines; Lives and practices in Shanghai, China
Rossana Hu: B. 1968 in Taiwan; Lives and practices in Shanghai, China

Reflective Nostalgia
Deep Thinking
Not Enough
Contextual
Quietness

"Architecture Makes Us Feel How We Touch the World and the World Touches Us"

In conversation with Juhani Pallasmaa, Architect and Critic

Email correspondence
in December 2020

B. 1936 in Hämeenlinna, Finland;
Lives and teaches in Helsinki,
Finland

Multisensory and
Existential Encounter

Authenticity of Human
Experience

Nuances and
Complexities

Special Atmosphere

Observations

I like your beautiful observations, particularly your poetic aphorism, "The door handle is the handshake of the building." What one building that you had a chance to visit gave you the biggest joy and what aspects make it special and memorable?

A building as a material structure is not the ultimate objective of architecture. In its very essence, architecture consists of mediating and dialogical relationships that make up the perception and experience of life. To me architecture is a verb; a meaningful building choreographing movements, actions, perceptions, and emotions that carry existential meanings. A building, which only exists as a detached aestheticized structure is not architecture; it is merely a utilitarian and economic investment. The task of architecture is to make our encounter with the world sensuous, intimate, and ennobling. Architecture is a multisensory and existential encounter, which mediates between the world and us. Architecture makes us feel how we touch the world and the world touches us.

One very special building for me is the Villa Mairea in western Finland, designed by Aino and Alvar Aalto and built in 1939. I have had the fortune of visiting it regularly since the late 1960s. It never fails in welcoming me with surprising generosity and freshness, as if I were opening its door for the first time. Every space, material, and detail all evoke curiosity and pleasure. This house contains endless unpredictable formal and emotive inventions and episodes, provoking endless imaginary narratives. It embraces, caresses, calms, and excites both the dweller and the visitor alike. The house invites you to get closer, to touch its countless details by eyes, skin, hands, and sense of self. It guides your interest to the forest around and the flowers in the garden, as well as the weather and the changing sunlight distilled through the proudly vertical pine trees. The house brings the rhythms and spatial densities of the forest indoors where the usual oppositions and polarities are merged. It makes one feel complete, balanced, and energized; the joy of inspiration and discovery is intoxicating and healing.

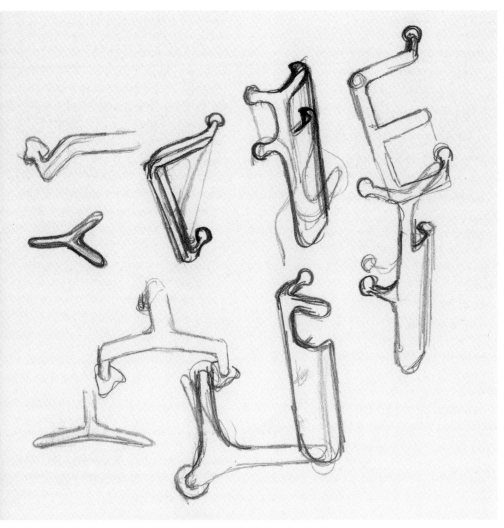

Portrait: Juhani Pallasmaa (photo © Knut Thyberg) **Above:** Juhani Pallasmaa, door handle
variations, prototypes (bronze, ebony, leather), 1991 (image courtesy Juhani Pallasmaa)

Portrait: Richard Pare at Color Space Imaging, New York, USA in 2012, examining his photo of Le Corbusier's Chapelle Notre-Dame du Haut at Ronchamp, France (1955) to be featured at *Le Corbusier: An Atlas of Modern Landscapes* exhibition at the Museum of Modern Art, MoMA in 2013 (photo © Richard Pare) **Above:** Vladimir Shukhov (engineer), The Shabolovka Tower, Moscow, Russia, 1922 (photo © Richard Pare, 2007) **Following pages:** Konstantin Melnikov, Architect's House in Krivoarbatsky Lane, Moscow, Russia, 1931 (photo © Richard Pare, diptych, 1998)

"A New Architecture for a New Age"

For about a decade—from the early 1990s to the early 2000s you frequently visited Russia and other former Soviet republics, documenting the most remarkable surviving examples of Russian Constructivism. Could you share that experience?

The idea of Russia has been in the back of my mind since childhood. Just after the collapse of the Soviet Union, the opportunity came at last to travel to Moscow. It soon became apparent that there was a rich subject in that still relatively unknown architecture of the modernist period from 1922 to 1932, the time when [Konstantin] Melnikov, [Moisei] Ginzburg, the [Alexander, Leonid, Viktor] Vesnin brothers, among others, had a moment, in which it was possible to build experimental structures that were a powerful symbol of the radical Socialist idea, a new architecture for a new age.

My project became a race against the destruction or ill-judged renovation of these structures. Nearly all the buildings still remained, though most were difficult to find and often in very dilapidated condition. Still, the energy of the architectural ideas persisted. I was concerned to communicate the extraordinary excitement that flourished for just a few years until the experiment was abruptly halted at the order of Joseph Stalin. The tragic aspect of a suppressed ideal, stifled before it truly flourished, was an inevitable subtext.

It became my mission to rebalance the record, to give the Russian avant-garde a more prominent place in the canon of the history of architecture in the twentieth century. I was trying to recapture the vigor and vivid experimentation that was so briefly present in the years immediately after the Revolution. This very rewarding project has resulted in an archive of many thousands of images on the subject that had scarcely been represented in all the fallow years, through which the buildings, large and small, had survived.

In conversation with
Richard Pare, Photographer

Photographer's printer in
New York, USA, July 9, 2007

B. 1948 in Portsmouth, UK; Lives
in Yorkshire near Richmond, UK;
works around the world

New Architecture for
New Society
Modernist Movement
Hope and Optimism
Independent Spirit
Spiritual Ease

"Everybody Can Share an Opinion, But at the End I'll Decide"

In conversation with Cesar Pelli of Pelli Clarke Pelli Architects, Architect

Architect's office in New Haven, Connecticut, USA, January 25, 2005

B. 1926 in San Miguel de Tucumán, Argentina; Lived in New York and New Haven, Connecticut, USA; practiced and taught in New Haven, Connecticut, USA

D. 2019 in New Haven, Connecticut, USA

Real Conditions and Restrictions
Architecture of Response
Tallness and Modernity
Marks in the City
Skyscrapers

Could you talk about your design process—rational versus intuitive, structure versus skin?

I don't believe that rational and intuitive are opposites. They are two aspects of the same thing and how we think. There is always intuition in every rational analysis and there is rational behind every intuitive aspect. We always begin with trying to understand rational aspects of a project: the site, the program, the codes, surrounded buildings, typography, winds, climate, etc. After all of these are congested, I will consider giving it a form. I think sketches that architects can't resist making while visiting the site are dreadful things. That is a weakness that we, architects, can't resist, but it is a bad habit because there is a danger that one can fall in love with a sketch and fall into a wrong direction.

Now, structure and skin. Both are very important. For centuries they used to be the same thing. The load-bearing wall was the structure and a coat of paint was its skin. But today in most buildings the skin is an element that surrounds the structure and is supported by the structure. So, there is a difference between structure and skin. The skin is what we see, but the structure is what gives the building order and form. I think all architects today treat the building's skin as a tablecloth. Our own skin doesn't represent our skeleton, but it depends on it. So, structure and skin have to have a dialogue.

Apart from the design, you must work with deadlines. I make all the decisions myself. But I listen to my colleagues carefully and, sometimes, I change my mind. Still, one person needs to make the decisions. We never argue. Everybody can share an opinion, but at the end I'll decide.

198

Portrait: Cesar Pelli (photo courtesy © Pelli Clarke Pelli Architects) **Above:** Pelli Clarke Pelli Architects, Petronas Towers, Kuala Lumpur, Malaysia, 1998 (photo courtesy © Pelli Clarke Pelli Architects)

Portrait: Renzo Piano (photo © Stefano Goldberg) **Above:** Renzo Piano Building Workshop, The Menil Collection, Houston, Texas, USA, 1981–87 (photo by Hickey & Robertson Photography © Piano & Fitzgerald, Architects, courtesy Fondazione Renzo Piano)

"Rationality Doesn't Sing; Intuition Does"

Beaubourg seems to be the most daring and provocative of all your buildings, such a revolution at the start of your career. It could never be built today, right?

I don't think about the Beaubourg. What keeps me going is not what I have done but what I will still do. We were lucky to be challenged with the right project at the right time. It symbolized that time, the time of great change, only a few years after the student riots of May 1968. You need a special moment for that. You need risk taking. If you only draw what you know you are going nowhere. If you don't find rebellion and energy within you then you can become totally paralyzed by just admiring what's already around you. When we are young, we need to find our own freedom, our own curiosity, our own imagination. You know, bread is like rationality and marmalade is like intuition. You can't have too much marmalade; you need to put it on bread. So, you need both—rationality and intuition to pursue your curiosity. But it is true that rationality doesn't sing; intuition does.

For me it was always about the process of building, modular construction, and achieving absolute economy. Modularity is about order. Life is always about order and disorder. Even a musician needs a pentagram to write notes. So, it was about anchoring my ideas in what is rational and clear. I admire people like Jean Prouvé who was concerned about inventing a system that would allow building architecture for everybody. It was a moral idea. Creative work is like looking in the dark. You need to be brave enough not to look for safe ground. Jorge Luis Borges said that imagination is made of memory and oblivion. Thank God we forget things, so we have our imagination to move forward. Creativity is always a mix of tradition and invention. The key message of this century is that the world is fragile. We simply can't build the way we used to. Nevertheless, more than anything, architecture is a search for beauty.

In conversation with Renzo Piano
of Renzo Piano Building
Workshop, Architect

Architect's office in New York,
USA, March 18, 2019

B. 1937 in Pegli, Italy;
Lives and practices in Paris,
France and Genoa, Italy

A Sense of Wonder,
Allusions, Feelings
Precision and Lightness
Order and Disorder
Mass Production
Modularity

"We Try to Slow Things Down"

In conversation with
Carme Pigem of RCR Arquitectes,
Architect

Architects' office in Olot near
Gerona, Catalonia, Spain,
November 29, 2019

B. 1962 in Olot, Catalonia, Spain;
Lives and practices in Olot,
Catalonia, Spain

Original, Sensual,
Personal, and Essential

Play with Nature and
with Materials

We Treat Spaces as
Artworks

A Special Feeling

Transformative

Thanks to you and some other architects, beauty has become one of the top qualities that ordinary people now associate with contemporary architecture, whereas for a good part of the twentieth century the public was disenchanted with modernist aesthetics, which were thought of as too cold and alienating. Is beauty your top priority?

All I can say is that solutions must be beautiful. It is on our mind all the time. Beauty for us is in the essentiality of things. How do we achieve beautiful architecture? Well, we have many rules, they are written on our walls. One of these rules is that when we find that a solution is not beautiful, we must continue looking for something better. [Laughs.]

Everything starts with understanding and reacting to the place and the problem. It is not about bringing what we already know. Otherwise, it will be out of place, irrelevant. We try to understand things and think of alternatives. And we are against the idea of working as professionals. That's not how we see ourselves. Because then you become a specialist. Meaning—you know what you are doing. Then there is no surprise, no experimentation anymore. Being a good professional means you know the right way, one and only way. That's not what we are interested in. We want to tackle problems to discover things. It gives us pleasure. It is not like we know what kind of building or image we want. We deal with the unknown. We like such process. We are interested in creating a new kind of space, new reality, new atmosphere. And when you encounter our spaces you never see everything at once. Intriguing, complex spaces absorb you and when you are absorbed, even the time seems to change, it slows down. This is important because we live in such fast-paced times. We work against that. We try to slow things down.

Portrait: Carme Pigem with Rafael Aranda (right) and Ramon Vilalta (left) of RCR Arquitectes (photo by Albert Beltran © RCR Bunka Fundacio) Above: RCR Arquitectes office, conference room within a garden, Barberi Space, Olot, 2006–ongoing (photo by Hisao Suzuki © RCR Bunka Fundacio)

Portrait: Christian de Portzamparc (photo © Richard Schulman) **Top & middle:** Christian de Portzamparc, Cidade Das Artes, Rio de Janeiro, Brazil, 2002–13 (photos © Hufton+Crow) **Bottom:** Christian de Portzamparc, Luxembourg Philarmonie, Luxembourg, 2005 (photo © Wade Zimmerman)

"No One Else But an Architect Can Solve the Problems of the Contemporary City"

In conversation with
Christian de Portzamparc,
Architect

When you won the Pritzker Prize in 1994, the Jury citation said, "Every architect who aspires to greatness must in some sense reinvent architecture." Is that something that you still try to do?

In the beginning I was constantly asking this question— what is architecture for? And I thought that an architect who is not asking this question is not an interesting architect. But reinventing is a very pretentious position. Instead, we recreate things through an intense dialogue between generations and ideas. We start again.

In 1965, I was under the impression that architects were obsolete. I thought the city of the future would be designed by sociologists and computers. Houses would be assembled in factories; people would buy what they like, and sociologists would assemble them. It would all become like a living process, just as Archigram and the Metabolists envisioned. I didn't want to become an engineer to assemble these plug-in cities.

To Le Corbusier, modernism was like Christianity to Saint Paul. There was no tolerance to anything that was existing before. I realized that if we have inherited this word "modern," the artistic banner of the twentieth century, its meaning is lost. This word cannot have the same meaning now as when Apollinaire declared one century ago, "I never want to stop being amazed by the locomotive." We cannot have the same basic experience that Le Corbusier had when asserting: "We, the first in history, saw the machine." The meaning of the word "modern" has to be reinvented. Modernism is a disruption in something existing and we live in an era of constant change and willingly or unwillingly architecture reinvents tomorrow from project to project. I believe that the best projects are about reinventing this confidence in the future. My main concern is in how to repair and continue building our cities. How to make them accessible and livable for everybody. No one else but an architect can solve the problems of the contemporary city.

Architect's studio in Paris,
France, November 14, 2016

B. 1944 in Casablanca, Morocco;
Lives and practices in Paris,
France

Communication Beyond
Language
A Drawing Could Be a
Place
Individual Character
A New City
Overture

"My Buildings Are Rides"

In conversation with
Antoine Predock, Architect

FaceTime video calls between
New York and Los Angeles, USA,
May 2 and 3, 2020

B. 1936 in Lebanon, Missouri,
USA; Lives and practices in
Albuquerque, New Mexico, USA

A Choreographic,
Physical, and
Intellectual Ride
Geological Formations
Poetic Encounter
Dance of Light
Kinesthetic

*You said, "In architecture you constantly have to make
stuff up." What is the role of imagination in your work?*

I have been a rider since high school and when I ride,
experience becomes seamless to me. My buildings are like
those rides. Architecture should be a ride—a choreographic,
physical, and intellectual ride. It is about feelings, emotions,
and experience. Architecture is an adventure, a fascinating
journey toward the unexpected. I want my buildings
to be experiential, like the Alhambra, where you realize
that the architecture is not about linear perspectival
order; it is rather about episodic spatial events, like a
movie storyboard or a Chinese scroll painting. Above all,
architecture is an Art, dwelling in imagination. Any building
must have a life of its own, independent of program, but
of course, accommodating the client's needs. Architecture
merely driven by program is soulless. My work is about
responding to place on the deepest level of understanding
and expressing it in the most powerful way. The design
experience must manifest the joy of invention and dream.
A building is not just what's standing there, it is a ride that
went into making it come alive.

When I come to a new place I want to know—what is the
wind direction? What are the climatic forces? When does
the sun rise and set on the summer solstice? What are the
geological underpinnings? I am interested in discovering
the cultural memory of a place, like in the writings of
Jorge Luis Borges or Federico Garcia Lorca. Architecture
is not just a theoretical game. Each building should be a
singular, unique event locked in time and place, and at the
same time a launchpad into the future. People have certain
expectations of what architecture is. I like to surprise
them. The point is not to produce a building, but a force,
charged with poetic power and conviction. The mission
of any architect is to have his deepest inner content made
visible through work.

Portrait: Antoine Predock (photo © Robert Reck, 2006) **Above:** Antoine Predock,
Canadian Museum for Human Rights, Winnipeg, Canada, 2014 (photo © Alex Fradkin)

Portrait: Wolf Prix (photo © Elfie Semotan) **Top:** Coop Himmelb(l)au, BMW Welt, Munich, Germany, 2001–07 (photo © Hélène Binet) **Bottom left:** Coop Himmelb(l)au, Akron Art Museum, Ohio, USA, 2001–07 (photo © Roland Halbe) **Bottom right:** Coop Himmelb(l)au, *The Cloud*, 1968, project (photo courtesy Coop Himmelb(l)au)

"Imagine Buildings Floating Like Clouds"

There is a passage in Moby Dick *that comes across in your writings: "I wish the wind had a body." Why do you dream about buildings floating like clouds?*

It is about changeable environment. It is not the building environment that should change human beings, but the human beings should be able to change the environment. In 1968, everything exploded. It was the time when students around the world went to the streets to demand change. Our motto was—power to the fantasy! We named ourselves Coop Himmelb(l)au (Cooperative Blue Sky), not after a color of the sky, but because we wanted to imagine buildings floating like clouds. Our very first project was called *The Cloud*. It was a fantasy project that imagined a new way of living in the future—pointing to such possibilities as creating interactive inflatable spaces that could be controlled with your heartbeat. We wanted to change our environment radically and now!

Starting in the mid-1970s we began working with the subconscious—by destroying the rational way of thinking in the moment of design, drawing with the eyes closed and other methods that could liberate space from rational and economic structure and refinement. In our projects we are working on forms, shapes, and images that are based on other things than just architecture. Unrestrained imagination is very important. Forget gravity, forget columns. We said: "Gravity? No, thank you!"

When I was 10 or 11 my father took me to the Kunsthistorisches Museum in Vienna and showed me the famous painting by Pieter Bruegel *The Tower of Babel*. I was thrilled by this picture, but it bothered me that the tower didn't have a spire. It was unfinished. I think the duty of every architect is to finish the Tower of Babel. But how could you want to finish the Tower of Babel if you are not a rebel? I still feel I want to change architecture!

In conversation with Wolf Prix of Coop Himmelb(l)au, Architect

Before Wolf Prix's lecture at Cooper Union in New York, USA, November 20, 2008

B. 1942 in Vienna, Austria; Lives, practices, and teaches in Vienna, Austria

I Want People to Remember My Buildings

Non-Architectural References

Form, Function, and Speed

Symbols for Open Society

Reality of Possibilities

"You Have to Go Beyond Limits"

In conversation with
Mauricio Rocha and
Gabriela Carrillo, Architects

Taller Rocha + Carillo studio in
Mexico City, Mexico, June 14, 2017

Mauricio Rocha: B. 1965 in Mexico
City, Mexico; Lives and practices
in Mexico City, Mexico

Gabriela Carrillo: B. 1978 in
Mexico City, Mexico; Lives and
practices in Mexico City, Mexico

Meaningful Silence,
Materiality, and
Melancholy
Intensity of Space and
Density of Light
Presence and Absence
Unarchitecture
Less Is Enough

*You said architecture is art. You do both; what makes
architecture art?*

MR: Only exceptional architecture is art. Once Tarkovsky
was asked about his favorite directors. He named several
who didn't just make good films, but who created their
own internal worlds that did not exist before—Kurosawa,
Fellini, Hitchcock, Bergman. The same with architecture.
There are only a few masters who were able to create their
own internal worlds—Wright, Le Corbusier, Mies, Kahn,
Barragan.

I love the work of Duchamp, particularly the story with
The Large Glass. It cracked during one of the moves and he
said—leave it like that, it is part of the piece. He made the
decision about the accident and accepted it as part of the
artwork. I learn from such things. I love making decisions
based on accidents. Every project is an opportunity. Every
project can bring a surprise.

GC: In a way, it is important not to doubt that architecture
is art. It is art because there is a need to go beyond
function; architecture is about provocation, emotion,
sensitivity. That's what art does.

When I studied architecture, my professor introduced
me to Mauricio's work, and I was drawn to his art
interventions even before I knew anything about his
architecture. I loved how his works fuse vernacular with
contemporary, how they offer an entirely new sensation of
experiencing space and going through it. To me his art was
architecture. What is important for us is to create a sense
of abstraction. Look at Michael Heizer's *Double Negative*,
the deep scars into the earth. To us that's space and
whether one calls it art or architecture that's irrelevant.
We like blurring boundaries and we want to make strong
buildings. Strong buildings are never about the first
impression.

Portrait: Mauricio Rocha and Gabriela Carrillo (photo © Rodrigo Navarro) **Top:** Taller Rocha + Carillo, Iturbide Studio, Mexico City, Mexico, 2017 (photo © Rafael Gamo) **Bottom:** Taller Rocher + Carillor, Iturbide Studio, Mexico City, Mexico, 2017 (sketch © Mauricio Rocha) Iturbide Studio is the home of well-known Mexican photographer Graciela Iturbide, Mauricio Rocha's mother. It was originally completed by Rocha in 1991. He opened his architecture studio in the house in 1998. The latest addition, a brick-screened courtyard, was finished in 2017.

Portrait: Moshe Safdie (photo by Michal Ronnen Safdie © Safdie Architects) **Above:** Habitat '67, Montreal, Quebec, Canada, 1967 (photo © Jade Doskow, *Lost Utopias* project, 2012)

"For Everyone a Garden"

Your very first project, Habitat '67, was an expression of your idealistic vision of a family living in the Israel of your childhood and the idea that you could build a multifamily housing project out of prefabricated units. How utopian was that vision?

It didn't quite work, but there was nothing utopian about that. What was utopian was the idea—for everyone a garden, even if it's on the 25th floor. That is now a reality, but how you build it has nothing to do with utopia. You just use the best building system available. If tomorrow someone invents a new material, a quarter the weight of concrete, and it is fireproof, I will be the first one to use it.

The project was driven by the memories of my childhood: the village settlements on Mount Carmel in Haifa, in northern Israel where I grew up. In my mind I had clustered Arab houses. The original Habitat was 25 stories high, supported by a huge megastructure. If that got built, I think, the impact would have been very different. What got built was the village. What didn't get built was the city. The original Habitat would include a school, shops, and so on. It was envisioned as a three-dimensional city. The key idea was to humanize high-density living, making it livable and enjoyable. The idea was to combine an urban model with the suburban one by stocking houses in a denser way.

Throughout my career I was inspired by Bernard Rudofsky's book and exhibition, *Architecture Without Architects* (MoMA), as well as D'Arcy Thompson's book on morphology, *On Growth & Form*. I am inspired by vernacular architecture because it is evolutionary. It is not invented. It adapts to the climate, the sun, the wind; it evolves. Future generations of architects will have to address the issues of higher densities, which has been the focus of my career—to establish a framework on the mega-scale of urban life.

In conversation with
Moshe Safdie, Architect

Architect's office in Somerville, near Boston, Massachusetts, USA, September 27, 2019

B. 1938 in Haifa, Israel; Lives and practices in Somerville near Boston, USA

To Humanize High-Density Living

Mega-Scale of Urban Life

Sensual and Uplifting

Conquering Light

Optimistic

"I Try and Make It More Fabulous Than What We See"

**In conversation with
Richard Schulman, Photographer**

Over lunch in Manhattan, New York, USA, January 22, 2021

B. 1954 in Los Angeles, California, USA; Lives in New York, USA; works around the world

Specificity of Bertolucci
The Narrative of Light
Life with the Camera
Another World
Flaneur

You once said you "hate" architects because "Architects rule the world. It is like The Matrix; they control the lives that we live. They determine everything about our cities, streets, buildings, even our own houses." Why don't you tell me what you love and what you are after as a photographer?

I have learned how to blur the lines between realist and fabulist. Essentially, I am the visual magical realist Gabriel García Márquez with a camera. My camera has been a documentary tool, capturing city life and the design of architecture as a cohesive frame of the lives we lead. Poverty and wealth have appeared in my pictures for 40 years. When I interpret architecture, I use my heart to tell a story about the banality and beauty of the wizardry of the built environment.

Of course, I said I "hate" architects facetiously. And I say that "architects rule the world," because the built environment encapsulates the movement of light and space in a narrative of the footprint of our universe. Structures are built for a permanence. But how we navigate our way across the urban planet is predicated on how the architects of the world utilize space. As a fabulist I want to take the words of Frank Gehry, Oscar Niemeyer, Tadao Ando, and a thousand other voices who have shared their ideas and agendas with me and spin them around in my neural network like the Rubik's Cube in full throttle and define the vocabulary of photography: space, light, science, math, and narration into one single frame. When I take a picture, I discover the light that defines the experience for me and share it with my mental archive of the photography of architecture's history. I then simply snap. Photography is one snap from one moment that reflects the present and is seen in the future as a capture of our past. Acting as a modern-day Aesop, I try and make it more fabulous than what we see.

Portrait: Richard Schulman
(photo © Barbara Schulman)
Above: 42nd Street, New York, USA,
1993 (photo © Richard Schulman)
Left: Christian de Portzamparc inside his
LVMH Tower on 57th Street, New York,
USA, 2004 (photo © Richard Schulman)
Following pages: Oscar Niemeyer,
The Niterói Contemporary Art Museum,
Rio de Janeiro, Brazil, 1996 (photo
© Richard Schulman)

"I Never Make Anything Hollow"

Everyone is intrigued by your Torqued Ellipses. *Where did the idea come from?*

I'll tell you. I was in Rome when I worked on conical sections and I walked into a Borromini's church San Carlo alle Quattro Fontane or San Carlino, as it is also known. And I saw that an oval on the floor and the dome above are misaligned. That was strange because Borromini was always perfect. So, I thought something was turned or shifted. But when I walked into the center, I realized it was an illusion and everything was perfectly aligned. Then I thought—what if I made a space embraced by a surface in such a way that at every elevation its radius would remain the same? The surface would lean in and out, but the radius would always be the same.

To make it I went to a nautical engineer that I knew, and I asked him to calculate such a surface for me. He said, "Look, this sounds very interesting but why don't you come next month when I'm not busy?" So, I started working on it by myself. I took two elliptical pieces of wood representing the void in the ceiling and the other piece of wood representing the elliptical void on the floor. I connected them with a dowel and twisted the ellipses to misalign them. Then I started to roll it on the floor to get the pattern that I was looking for and wrap it around the ellipses. I used lead to play with the surface because it is the most pliable and easy to work with material. Then I went back to the same engineer and showed him my pattern. He said, "Did you use any computer program?" Then I told him how I did it and he said, "OK, I can work with you on this. Come tomorrow." That's how we did it. So, this shape is not going to change the world, but it is an invention. And all my pieces are solid. I never make anything hollow. I'm interested in mass and weight, and the loadbearing and gravitational feel of what that means. You now, you can make things appear weightless, even floating, simply by placing them in certain ways?!

In conversation with
Richard Serra, Artist

Gagosian Gallery in New York,
USA, May 24, 2006

B. 1938 in San Francisco, California,
USA; Lives and works in Tribeca,
New York, USA and on the North
Fork, Long Island, New York, USA

I Want to Exceed My
Own Language
Weights and
Counterweights
Body Movement
Process
Gravity

"Beauty Is the Top of Functionality!"

In conversation with Álvaro Siza, Architect

Architect's office in Porto, Portugal, December 10, 2016

B. 1933 in Matosinhos, Portugal; Lives and practices in Porto, Portugal

Architecture Is Art, or It Is Not Architecture

Drawing Is as Essential as Breathing

Rationality Is Not Enough

Free of All Constraints

Nothing Is Invented

Eduardo Souto de Moura said, "Siza's houses are just like cats sleeping in the sun." Could you talk about your buildings in relation to their sites and the role of drawing as a design tool?

[Laughs.] Yes, he meant that my buildings assume the most natural postures on the site. There is also a reference to the human body. Drawing is very important. Even before I have complete knowledge, or good knowledge of every single problem, I begin sketching possible solutions with the little information I have. I feel I need to begin immediately with an idea—although then it can be completely changed. I don't worry about analyzing the problem, the site conditions, or even the program. Because if I first do all the analysis there would be too much information and little architecture. So first, I sketch, sometimes before I go to the site. I immediately start searching for an idea, even if I only have a photo of the place. And most of the time the first sketches are good for nothing. But I use them to construct an idea that comes out of many sketches. Gradually, with more information, a real thing emerges. My collaborators will feed me with information. I work with models directly and at some point—the rigor that comes from precise information and complete freedom of my intuition—will meet.

What I am most interested in is beauty. Beauty is the top of functionality! If something is beautiful, it is functional. I don't separate the two. Beauty is the key functionality for architects. It should be the number one preoccupation of any architect. Yet, architecture is a service. Architects have an ethical responsibility to deliver a project that responds to a particular set of objectives as rigorously as possible. Still, architecture should remain free. Rationality is not enough. I want to go around the problem. When architecture is in search for beauty it is art, as much as painting, sculpture, cinema, music. Everyone understands beauty differently. To me beauty is what I see as something authentic. Authenticity is beautiful.

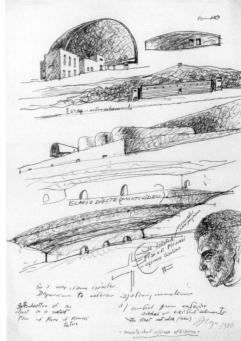

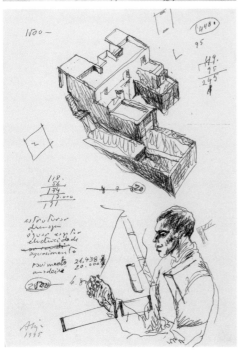

Portrait: Álvaro Siza (photo courtesy Álvaro Siza Arquitecto)
Top left: Álvaro Siza, sketch for the rectorate building of the
University of Alicante, Spain, 1995, pencil on black-and-white copy,
294 x 210 mm (sketch © Álvaro Siza, courtesy Tchoban Foundation,
Museum of Architectural Drawing, Berlin) **Top right:** Álvaro Siza,
sketches for the residential complex Quinta da Malagueira, Évora,
Portugal, 1980, ballpoint pen, paper, 297 x 210 mm (image © Álvaro
Siza, courtesy Tchoban Foundation, Museum of Architectural
Drawing, Berlin) **Left:** Álvaro Siza, sketches for Casa Pinto Sousa
and portrait of Júlio Silva, 1995, ballpoint pen, paper, 297 x 210 mm
(image © Álvaro Siza, courtesy Tchoban Foundation, Museum of
Architectural Drawing, Berlin)

Portrait: Michael Sorkin (photo courtesy Michael Sorkin) **Above:** Michael Sorkin Studio, *Weed City*, Yuma, Arizona, USA, 1994 (image courtesy Michael Sorkin Studio) **Right:** Michael Sorkin Studio in collaboration with Terreform 1, New York 2106: Self Sufficient City (image courtesy Michael Sorkin Studio)

"I'm Interested in How You Start a City"

In conversation with
Michael Sorkin, Architect,
Critic, and Urbanist

Michael Sorkin Studio in
Manhattan, New York, USA,
August 9, 2007

B. 1948 in Washington D.C., USA;
Lived, practiced, and taught in
New York, USA

D. 2020 in Manhattan,
New York, USA

Building an
Imaginative City
A Sense of History
Urban Fantasies
Walkable Cities
Tolerance

What prompted your interest in urbanism? Will we ever build an ideal city?

I had an interest in cities from a very young age. My mother, a social worker, gave me *The City in History* by Louis Mumford in 1961, the year it was published. I was enthralled. The book connected my interests in social issues and the morphological developments of cities. Mumford had a great passion for cities as incubators of democratic social life and believed that forms transmitted values. For years I dreamed of visiting a new modernist city, Vallingby, a suburb of Stockholm, showcased as an ideal and sustainable town, but it turned out to be a very dull place when I finally visited it years later. Nevertheless, I'm an old-fashioned utopian, and I strongly believe in the necessity to invent and build self-sufficient cities from scratch, as opposed to continuing the expansion of urban texture and increasing the density of existing cities.

Part of my "mission" is to keep the spirit of the avant-garde alive by pushing students to be curious and inventive. I emphasize different possibilities for self-sustaining and self-sufficient, walkable cities that rely on their local resources. One of the markers of a good city is that you can get lost in it. I love and I learn a lot from Prague, Siena, Venice, Fez, Cairo, Calcutta, and Kyoto. Indian and Japanese cities in particular are thick with stimuli. And who doesn't love Paris? Cities invent architecture. They are the source of architecture's meaning. The big topic, of course, is how architecture and urbanism are going to contribute to the survival of the planet and to assure a safe, fair, and fulfilling life for everybody. Every architect must be an urbanist, because inescapably this is an urban planet now.

I'm interested in how you start a city, how you continue a city, how you complete a city, how you judge a city. Yet, I think the idea of imagining something ideal and perfect is dangerous. And I think architecture tends to get into trouble when there is a monolithic theory describing its own production. I'm interested in lively debate and let the best theory win, but just for a while. Let 1,000 urban theories bloom!

"I Look Beyond Solution; I Look for an Expression"

Interview with Eduardo
Souto de Moura, Architect

Architect's studio in Porto,
Portugal, November 10, 2016

B. 1952 in Porto, Portugal;
Lives and practices in
Porto, Portugal

Beauty Is in
Contradictions
Sensation of Simplicity
An Object Is Enough
No Narrative
Tension

Your book, Floating Images: Eduardo Souto de Moura's
Wall Atlas *is full of your sketches, photos of ruins, medieval
towers, aircraft carriers, offshore oil platforms, ads of elegant
dresses, newspaper and magazine clippings, and so on. What
role do these images play in your work?*

Very direct. It is like a flash, no intention. I see something
intriguing and that sparks my interest. I don't think about
it. If I like an image, I keep it and I might use it, or I may
never use it. I once recognized a project by Frank Gehry in
a photo of a fire in China. There is a connection between
images and projects. But I don't like explaining how the
process works; it is not rational. If you try to explain
your intentions, you are lying. Architecture is all about
copying. We copy the things we see. When this copying
process happens consciously it is a disaster. It should be
subconscious, almost unintentional. When I am working,
these images come up. I look beyond solution; I look for
an expression. I also collect phrases. For example, I like
Freud's, "From error to error one discovers the entire
truth." Another one is by Beckett, "Ever tried. Ever failed.
No matter. Try Again. Fail again. Fail better." So, the
intention is always the same—to try to find something
special and personal.

What makes architecture is beautiful details. They may
not be functional, they may not be truthful, but if they are
beautiful, they are essential. As Nietzsche said, "We have
art in order not to die of the truth." Beauty is necessary
to be pursued but it is not necessary for the building to
stand up or perform its function. If you cut a slice of any
building and see what's on the outside and what's holding
it, you will see no relation. The truth is buried underneath.
You can't be straightforward in architecture. You need to
be inventive to achieve something beautiful. To achieve the
sensation of simplicity I need to invent layers of complexity
behind it.

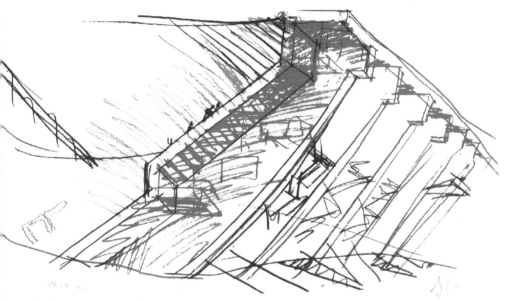

Portrait: Eduardo Souto de Moura (photo © Sofia Moro) **Above:** Sketch by Eduardo Souto de Moura,
Municipal Stadium, Braga, Portugal, 2003 (sketch courtesy Eduardo Souto de Moura)

Portrait: Frank Stella in an expandable foam rubber hat from Rio, Brazil (photo © Art Resource, NY)
Above: Frank Stella, *Takht-i-Sulayman I*, 1967, synthetic polymer paint on canvas, The Museum of Modern Art, New York © Frank Stella/Artists Rights Society (ARS), New York

"A Sculpture Dies Every Night"

Your work has evolved from paintings to wall reliefs to freestanding sculptures that extended into architecture. What is it that attracts you to architecture?

It is not a question of my attraction to architecture, but it is the form making that really attracts me. I love making forms. I don't think there is much of a difference. It should all be the same thing—painting, sculpture, and architecture. Le Corbusier did everything and what couldn't Michelangelo do? Yet, I think there are more possibilities within architecture and there are more reasons for consistency. As a sculptor, I want to go beyond the idea of modularity or just black and white palette, but architecture has so many more variables—play of planes, forms, light, and shadows— all changing with the time of day and with seasons, and in relation to the environment. There are plenty of aspects to explore just visually and aesthetically, apart from so many functional aspects. But a sculpture dies every night. Sculptures are singular objects, whereas a building is typically a part of other buildings and so many other elements in the city, and the city is always changing.

Ultimately, I think a lot has to do with the relationships among various parts. But more importantly, a work of art has to possess an aesthetic quality, it has to be beautiful. Isn't it beauty that motivates artists to keep working? If the work of art is beautiful nothing else matters. And it is true that each artist and each architect has a very different understanding of beauty, but that doesn't bother me. What matters is that I know that something is beautiful. I believe I have a fundamental sense of structure. I can tell when pieces are together or falling apart. To me, an artwork has to be visually stable. And what is most interesting to me, it is to push something as far as you can, out of balance. This is true about all works of art both from our time and from the past. And the point is not to come up with variations and repetitions. The point is to come up with something entirely new.

In conversation with
Frank Stella, Artist

Artist's studio in Manhattan,
New York, USA, August 9, 2012

B. 1936 in Malden,
Massachusetts, USA;
Lives in SoHo,
New York, USA

From a Painting to an
Object
Stability—Instability
Against a System
Delightfulness
Abstraction

"A City Is Like a Play in a Theater"

In conversation with
Sergei Tchoban of SPEECH,
Architect

Hôtel Ritz Paris in Paris, France,
November 12, 2016

B. 1962 in Saint Petersburg, Russia;
Lives and practices in Berlin,
Germany; and Moscow and Saint
Petersburg, Russia

Urban Mise-en-scène
Situations
Harmony of Contrasts
Richness of Details
Hierarchy of Roles
Context

Could you talk about the role of drawing in your architecture?

Drawing should be the key to understanding architecture—what is there to like or dislike and where do architects' ideas come from? In my passion for architecture, I am guided primarily by cities and urban mise-en-scène situations that I enjoy most, and the ones that I really like, I immediately try to capture on paper. I have a very straightforward attitude toward architecture. I always ask one simple question—would I want to draw one of my own projects or my colleagues' projects? This criterion may seem frivolous, but, in fact, it is quite rigorous.

My architecture emerges out of my drawings. I travel a lot and I spend a lot of time drawing. I am interested in the fabric of historical cities, details of individual buildings, and contrasts occurring when historical and contemporary layers overlap. For me a city is like a play in a theater and my buildings perform different roles. There are ordinary buildings and extraordinary ones that perform leading roles. Architects should also know well how to design ordinary buildings. There must be a hierarchy of roles. Not all roles should be the leading ones.

We are free not to look at paintings, but we cannot avoid looking at architecture; architecture should be beautiful. I associate beauty with such notions as tension, complexity, and contradiction. Moreover, such a definition as contrasting harmony also impresses me a lot, since the harmony of contradictions and not only similarities could be considered beautiful and a part of the search for an attractive artistic gesture.

Portrait: Sergei Tchoban (photo by Holger Talinski © Sergei Tchoban) **Top left:** Sergei Tchoban, Architectural fantasy for the Museum for Architectural Drawing in Berlin, Germany, charcoal and pencil on paper (410 x 310 mm), 2010 (drawing © Sergei Tchoban) **Top right:** Sergei Tchoban, *Grand Tower III, Monument or Excursion to the Monument* (from the series "Totalitarianism and Architecture"), sepia, watercolor and ink on paper (865 x 612 mm), 2016 (drawing © Sergei Tchoban) **Bottom:** Sergei Tchoban, *House for Bosch*, Polytych, sepia on paper (230 x 310 mm), 2016 (drawing © Sergei Tchoban)

Portrait: Stanley Tigerman (photo courtesy Tigerman McCurry Architects) **Above:** Stanley Tigerman, *The Titanic* (Mies van der Rohe's Crown Hall sinking into Lake Michigan), 1978 (image courtesy Tigerman McCurry Architects)

"I Am an American Architect; I Am a Hybrid"

You were a founding member of the postmodernist group, the Chicago Seven, which started in 1976. What were its main intentions and legacy?

Imagine that time—Mies died in 1969. The Miesians, his followers, took over Chicago and most modern buildings were built as Mies would do them—with the expression of the structural grid. There was no room for anything else, for people like me or anyone who was not a follower of Mies. So, we did a book and a show on Chicago architects. And unlike the New York Five or the Grays, we were not cohesive. We were working in all possible directions. We were not even good friends. But we wanted to open up the city because it wasn't open to us. We wanted to open it to the next generation.

America is a hybrid. This is not our home, unless you are a Native American. Nobody is from here. So, you are automatically alienated here. I wrote a book called *The Architecture of Exile* on this subject. There are no American architectural symbols; the technology—yes, of course, that's what Mies understood so well. But for symbolism, we have to look elsewhere. For example, postmodernism was an American movement because it is a hybrid movement, not authentic.

Architecture is a very difficult pursuit. You have to be strong to get something built. We had a meeting today here and everybody was trying to put an obstacle in front of me. Why? Because I am trying to do something that was never done before. And there is always a resistance to that, inertia. Try to build even a little cottage in a virgin forest and all the environmentalists will go against you because you are doing something that was not intended to be there. So, making a new building requires a great strength, immense will, fortitude, belief. Architecture is for tough guys. John Hejduk said it all, "The closer the finished building to the original drawing the better the building is." But it is very hard to do that because buildings get attacked and often lose their poetic content.

In conversation with
Stanley Tigerman, Architect

Architect's office in Chicago, USA,
April 17, 2012

B. 1930 in Edgewater near
Chicago, USA; Lived, practiced,
and taught in Chicago, USA

D. 2019 in Chicago, USA

Buildings with a Sense
of Irony
Pleasure and Humour
(Dis)Order
Allegory
Aura

"I Believe in Placing Architecture in the Realm of Ideas and Invention"

In conversation with
Bernard Tschumi, Architect

Architect's office in New York,
USA, January 2, 2004

B. 1944 in Lausanne, Switzerland;
Lives, practices, and teaches in
New York, USA and Paris, France

Challenge the Limits of
Architecture
Spatial Dynamics and
Movements
Cinematic Experience
Form Follows Fiction
Radical Questioning
Beyond Clichés

*Who, in your view, was the first architect to use
deconstructivist ideas in architecture?*

Well, it is hard for me to name one person. You have
Frank Gehry who is using a bricolage of materials in a
very liberated way and then later uses computer software,
which allows him to do complex curvilinear geometry.
You have Peter Eisenman who develops an obsessive
formal investigation and theoretical and philosophical
discourse. You have Coop Himmelb(l)au who in a very
intuitive way, in the early 1970s, is testing collisions,
distortions, tensions, and compressions in materials. You
have Rem Koolhaas who is fascinated with Leonidov and
Russian Constructivists, and with technology as a way of
introducing a new vocabulary. You have Daniel Libeskind
who is interested in symbolism. You have Zaha Hadid who
has an incredible intuition in purely formal issues. And I
am interested in literary theory, new social programs, and
film theory. For example, my Parc de la Villette in Paris was
conceived as the cinematic promenade, analogous to a
film strip. Architecture is always about movement, ideas,
and events within. I believe in placing architecture in the
realm of ideas and invention.

So, I took you chronologically at who was first developing
certain things, but we were all different. Yet, I believe, what
we were doing then we were working in the spirit of that
period. We all knew each other by teaching together at the
Architectural Association in London and at the New York's
Institute for Architecture and Urban Studies. But there
was no one person to influence the others. Or maybe
everybody influenced everybody.

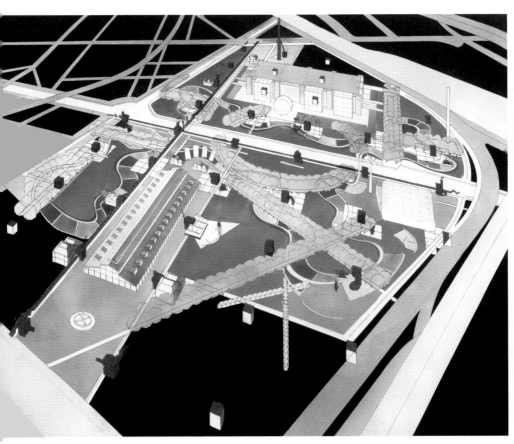

Portrait: Bernard Tschumi (photo © Bernard Tschumi Architects, 2006) **Above:** Bernard Tschumi,
Parc de la Villette, Paris, France, 1983–98 (rendering © Bernard Tschumi Architects)

Portrait: Lin Utzon (photo © Jean Marie del Moral) **Above:** Lin Utzon, *Cosmic dance II*, Fondazione Cini, 2016 Venice Architecture Biennale (photo © Thomas Mølvig)

"You Are Born with Your Song"

Your work has a very strong hand. Did you go through a long search period and was there a particular influence on your work by your father?

I think you are born with your song. Also, you try all your life to escape your song. It is hard. My work is very strong and heavy. Perhaps I would like to explore something lighter. What I am striving for is the ethereal and the eternal, which, of course, is unattainable. Sometimes, I want to make something so light it could float. But I can't. It doesn't come out that way. This is how I express myself.

I wouldn't say I was particularly influenced by anyone. I wouldn't say that I am influenced by my father directly, and yet, I am totally influenced by my father because of the kind of house I grew up in. I love modern architecture and adore the vitality that his buildings have. But, more importantly, there was always a prevailing creative force around me and my brothers that my father was the primary exponent of.

It was the environment I grew up in that defined who I've become. We lived in a house, which my father himself had built, in the middle of a forest, in a tiny village, and the life was oriented toward creating. If I wanted to have a sandpit in the house, I built the sandpit. I could collect feathers and leaves and decorate or paint the house however I wanted. There was real openness in our home, and already as a child, I was inspired by space and I could always express myself artistically. It was great because my father was very positive. Anything was possible! I was never told what to do and I always had my head sort of in the clouds—very fortunate.

When I moved to Spain and set up my own studio there my father was very interested in my work and our relationship was often more like between two artists. He started painting and doing collages in his later years. I would like to believe that I influenced his decision to start that. It was fantastic to be around him because he believed that anything is possible.

In conversation with
Lin Utzon, Artist

Artist's home in Hellebæk,
Denmark, September 29, 2012

B. 1946 in Copenhagen, Denmark;
Lives and practices in Hellebæk,
Denmark and Mallorca, Spain

The Mystery of Things
Anything Is Possible
Cosmic Dance
Solitude
Vitality

"We Gladly Acknowledge the Ordinary and the Culture and Symbolism of Everyday"

In conversation with Robert Venturi and Denise Scott Brown, Architects

Venturi, Scott Brown and Associates, Inc. office in Philadelphia, USA, July 16, 2004

Robert Venturi: B. 1925 in Philadelphia, USA; Lived, practiced, and taught in Philadelphia, USA

D. 2018 in Philadelphia, USA

Denise Scott Brown: B. 1931 in Nkana, Zambia; retired from practice in 2012; lives in Philadelphia, USA

Signage and Symbolism
Elements of Layering
Ugliness and Beauty
Breaking the Order
Historical Analogy

Critics say your Vanna Venturi House is the most significant house of the second half of the twentieth century because it is the first postmodernist house. Do you agree?

RV: I think it is the first Modern house that employs symbolic references. It says, "I'm a house; I'm a shelter." Modernists would never do that. On the other hand, I love the Villa Savoye by Le Corbusier and I learned a lot from it. It also employs symbolism, but industrial symbolism, within, ironically, its abstract aesthetic.

I think postmodernism involves a complete misunderstanding. We have nothing to do with it. In *Complexity and Contradiction*, I employed references to historical architecture for purposes of comparative analysis. But historical architecture should be analyzed not copied. I think there is nothing wrong in employing historical reference, but there should be no ambiguity about what is historical and what is contemporary.

DSB: I think the Vanna Venturi House did influence what architects call postmodernism. But architects misunderstood its direction, what it stood for. For me, it has in it, in embryo, almost everything we have done since. If you look at our later projects, such as the Sainsbury Wing in London, you can find Vanna Venturi House in there. So, its roots are important for our own subsequent work. And since it was built, it has served as a touchstone for the ideas of successive generations of architects. This is more important than its temporary distortion by postmodernists. We said, "Hey, we can learn from this. We are not only going to learn from Le Corbusier, but also from what is considered the ordinary." We gladly acknowledge the ordinary and the culture and symbolism of everyday.

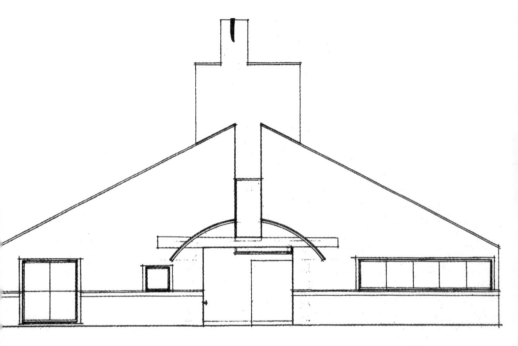

Portrait: Robert Venturi and Denise Scott Brown (photo © Matt Wargo, 2010, courtesy Venturi, Scott Brown and Associates, Inc.)
Above: Venturi, Scott Brown and Associates, Inc., Vanna Venturi House, Philadelphia, Pennsylvania, USA, 1964 (sketch by Robert Venturi, courtesy Venturi, Scott Brown and Associates, Inc.)

Portrait: Massimo Vignelli (photo courtesy Massimo Vignelli) **Above:** Massimo Vignelli, Heller Stackables, 1972 (photo courtesy Vignelli Associates)

"If You Solved a Problem You Made a Statement!"

In conversation with
Massimo Vignelli, Designer

What in your view is the difference between design and art and between design and architecture?

Design is not art because the more there is art the less there is design. Good design helps to solve a problem, but art is not there to solve problems. When design becomes too artistic it really suffers. Design is utilitarian, whereas art is useful but not utilitarian. One of my main desires is to decrease the amount of vulgarity around by replacing it with things that are more refined.

Design and architecture are much closer. Architecture has a component of complexity and permanence. Architecture is a lot more complex than design. But what I try to stay away from in my design is being trendy and fashionable. It should be more about problem-solving and targeting at being timeless and not stylized or ephemeral.

I think good architecture should last forever. Good design should last forever. I am not looking for developing a personal style in design. I don't have a cult of personality, but I do have a cult of objectivity. Subjectivity is very irritating. I love the work of Jonathan Ive, the designer behind all Apple products who has done a fabulous job by looking for objectivity and staying away from subjectivity. I think Ive is the best designer in the world today.

In my own work, I never pretend to be an artist. I don't believe that good design is a commentary on everyday life or the real world. I think there are so many other ways to make a comment or a statement. You can write, play, perform. I don't think a chair should be a comment. A chair should not be a capricious sculpture. It should be about how comfortable it is to sit in. So, how do we balance between solving a problem and making a statement? Well, if you solved a problem you made a statement!

Designer's home studio in
Manhattan, New York, USA,
February 10, 2012

B. 1931 in Milan, Italy; Lived and
practiced in New York, USA

D. 2014 in Manhattan,
New York, USA

Complex But Not
Complicated
Fight Against Ugliness
Intellectually Elegant
Responsible Attitude
Visually Powerful

"Imagine Bridges and Terraces in the Sky!"

In conversation with
Rafael Viñoly, Architect

Architect's office in New York,
USA, May 2008

B. 1944 in Montevideo,
Uruguay; Lives and practices in
New York, USA

Architecture Is a
Compositional Business

Unique Urban
Experiment

Control Over
Proportions

Moments of Freedom

Subtleties

As a New Yorker and finalist for the World Trade Center redevelopment, do you have any particular philosophy about tall buildings?

I think it is hard not to have a position or philosophy about tall buildings while living and practicing architecture in a city like New York. It is a unique urban experience. The basic planning strategy—the grid is probably the most ingenious planning device anywhere in the world. The genius of the grid is in the fact that it absorbs all possible growth and maintains the right balance. The city is not shaped by esthetical decisions. It works like an incredible mechanism and there is no conflict in losing unity because it is in this perpetual mode of evolving. Everything is very pragmatic and there is beauty and harmony in that too. I like to compare tall buildings to bridges, because to me they represent infrastructure and a way of inventing new types of accessible public space. They are public structures. Imagine bridges and terraces in the sky! Cities depend on very strong gestures, ideas, and people who know how to go forward. It is so essential in our cities to celebrate bird's-eye views. It is such a memorable, unique and absolutely essential experience in the twenty-first-century metropolis. Also, architecture cannot be dogmatic. There is no right or wrong. It all depends on how you do it. What is inherited in high-rise construction is simply critical for survival—solving increasing density issues. Skyscraper development is a natural and healthy phenomenon. The question is not about height but—how you maintain the survivability of a city past the point when there is a danger of it becoming an open-air museum. It is very important to have the right criteria for new developments, which are essential for urban life, but not from the perspective of acquiring buildings like prestigious trophies. Rather, it should be important to think how these buildings can be increased and be sustainable.

Portrait: Rafael Viñoly (photo by Lucas Michael, courtesy Rafael Viñoly Architects) **Top left:** Rafael Viñoly Architects, Tokyo International Forum, Tokyo, Japan, 1996 (photo © Akio Kawasumi) **Top right:** Rafael Viñoly Architects, 432 Park Avenue, New York, USA, 2015 (photo by Halkin Mason, courtesy Rafael Viñoly Architects) **Bottom:** Rafael Viñoly Architects, Carrasco International Airport, Montevideo, Uruguay, 2009 (photo © Daniela Mac Adden)

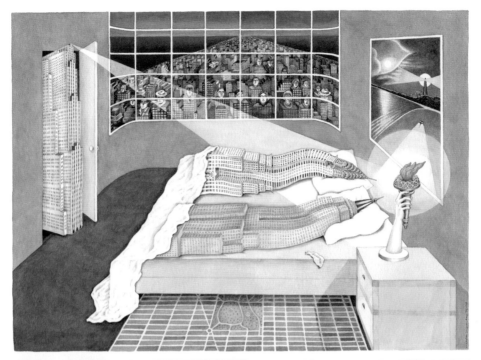

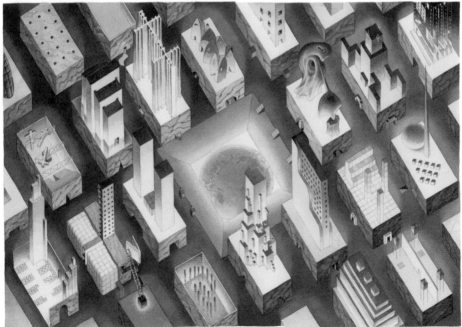

Portrait: Madelon Vriesendorp (photo © Charlie Koolhaas, Daughter) Top: Madelon Vriesendorp, *Flagrant Délit*, watercolor and gouache, 60 x 50 cm, 1975 (image courtesy Madelon Vriesendorp) Bottom: Madelon Vriesendorp, *The City of the Captive Globe* (Revised), watercolor, 56 x 39 cm, 1994 (image courtesy Madelon Vriesendorp)

"I Have Been Building an Alternative Life for Myself"

Could you share some of the original ideas behind your vision of presenting buildings like people and showing the secret life of buildings in your urban scenes of Manhattan?

It was about depicting buildings built in New York in the 1920s and 1930s, the art deco period, when celebrity culture was thriving, and architecture was a part of it. Architects were designing iconic objects for cities. Buildings competed at being the tallest, which humanized them, in a way, and brought humor into architecture. I love Saul Steinberg's brilliant cartoons and collages of skyscrapers done in the early 1970s, when I was doing my series of New York paintings and Rem [Koolhaas] was writing his *Delirious New York*. As we were going around collecting material for his book—postcards and books on NYC—I discovered other subjects and started collecting little buildings, souvenirs, figures, toys, etc. It became a real obsession. It was like creating an alternative life for myself, a visual counterpoint to the formal architectural debate. It's a sort of escapism from reality, isn't it? But it was also a way to get inspired and maybe inspire others. As Thomas Edison observed, "To invent you need a good imagination and a pile of junk." [Laughs].

"The City of the Captive Globe" was a chapter in Rem's book, explaining the idea of the grid, generating blocks and thus allowing different ideologies to exist side by side where new connections and relationships could be forged. His enthusiasm inspired my paintings. For the revised version of *The City of the Captive Globe* I sneaked a skeletal version of his entry for the Paris Grande Bibliothèque competition in the upper right corner.

And so, we inspired each other, traveled together, met all kinds of people, and kept collecting anything that could expand our mindset and prove Rem's theories. I like to say that I don't believe in authenticity: we borrow and steal from everything we absorb. Every time I visit a new city, I go straight to the hardware store, toy store, and maritime museum. That's the most direct way to understand the local culture.

In conversation with
Madelon Vriesendorp, Artist

WhatsApp video call,
January 29, 2021

B. 1945 in Bilthoven, near Utrecht,
The Netherlands; Lives and works
in London, UK

Secret Life of Buildings
Delirious New York
Imaginary Worlds
Clash of Cultures
Dream-Like

"My Biggest Inspiration Is a Bamboo Forest"

In conversation with
Vo Trong Nghia of VTN Architects,
Architect

Viber audio call between New York, USA and Ho Chi Minh City, Vietnam, October 13, 2020

B. 1976 in Phú Thủy, Quảng Bình, Vietnam; Lives and practices in Ho Chi Minh City, Vietnam

Healthy Lifestyle
Sense of Peace
Meditation
Calmness
Serenity

You are known for introducing greenery into architecture and connecting people to nature. Could you talk about the key principles of your work?

Vietnamese cities lost their tropical beauty. They have turned into concrete jungles. It is very clear—without nature around us we become crazy, quite literally. What we try to do as architects is to wrap nature around our lives. We want to reintroduce greenery back into our cities, to reconnect people and nature, and use plants as a building material to integrate vernacular wisdom into modern architecture. I love trees and forests. I love the idea of living under a tree. I always dreamed about living in a house that would feel like being in the middle of a forest. Each one of our buildings can serve as a small park for the city ... I would say that my biggest inspiration is a bamboo forest.

Bamboo can replace timber, concrete, and even steel. We use it structurally to form arches and domes. I think bamboo can, and will, replace other materials to become the "green steel" of the twenty-first century. We also get our inspirations from smaller objects—fruit baskets, fish baskets, even chicken cages. I love playing with different scales in my work ... Other influences come from the work of my professor at Tokyo University, Hiroshi Naito, in my view, the best architect in Japan today. Another reference is a building I visited in Fukuoka, ACROS Centre by Emilio Ambasz. But my criticism of it is that once you go inside you lose all relation to the greenery. The landscape is beautiful, but inside it is a conventional building. Still, it is very inspiring, and I saw its potential right away. Green architecture is not just about wrapping a building with a landscape, but to provide a different kind of quality. How do you bring nature into a building? How do you benefit from nature and enjoy space inside? The way people live is a lot more important to me than an abstract idea or image. Green means being friendly with the environment, not just planting trees. We have a mission—to bring greenery into all our projects. I want to create a new language of architecture for our country.

Portrait: Vo Trong Nghia (photo courtesy VTN Architects) **Above:** VTN Architects, House for Trees, Tan Binh District, Ho Chi Minh City, Vietnam, 2014 (photo © Hiroyuki Oki)

Portrait: Wang Shu and Lu Wenyu (photo © Iwan Baan) Top: Amateur Architecture Studio, Xiangshan Campus, China Academy of Art, Hangzhou, China, Phase II, 2004-07 (photo © Iwan Baan) Bottom: Amateur Architecture Studio, Xiangshan Campus, China Academy of Art, Hangzhou, China, Phase II, 2004, sketch by Wang Shu from left to right without stopping—duration four hours (sketch courtesy Amateur Architecture Studio)

"Achieving Good Architecture Is Like Flying a Kite"

Your Ningbo Museum diffuses a notion of a single authorship. Could you talk about diversity, anonymity, and multiplicity of voices in your architecture?

I pursued this concept of anonymity in my PhD at Tongji University. This is what you can see in traditional houses in Suzhou—they are delightful and beautiful, but not in a personal way. They are a product of a very organic language. That is what's moving about these structures. And that's what I was trying to express in a different way, in the Ningbo Museum. I call this building's façades—architecture completed by one thousand hands. I refer to the diversity of techniques in the building's construction. And we mixed new and salvaged materials side by side. I wanted to build a small town with its own life, which could wake up the latent memory of the city that was built over the demolished ancient villages on the site.

The success in Ningbo was in achieving the right balance between the architects intervening too much and letting the workers be free, to a point. Achieving good architecture is like flying a kite. There is always a string attached to the building process. I would like to call the result of the Ningbo History Museum an anthropological fact in existence. Every time I am building a building the intention is to create a world and a path that leads us back to nature. Getting lost in this world is a recurring theme in my work.

The essence of my architecture is in trying to maintain a cultural continuity. You can't protect and preserve culture as is. That is not enough. You have to find a dialogue between tradition and continuously changing life. Each generation has its own understanding of traditions. It is important to be conscious that all of us are taking part in re-composing traditions as we know them—in how we carry on different stories or re-compose and interpret the language. We may not be aware of it, but we are continuously re-composing the reality we know.

In conversation with
Wang Shu of Amateur
Architecture Studio, Architect

WeChat video call between
New York, USA and Hangzhou,
China, October 23, 2020

B. 1963 in Ürümqi, Xinjiang, China;
Lives, practices, and teaches in
Hangzhou, China

Anonymity of One
Thousand Hands
Breathable and
Salvaged Materials
Countryside
Resistance
Garden

247

"A Vase May Give
a Shape to a Room"

In conversation with
John Wardle, Architect

Skype video call between
New York, USA and Melbourne,
Australia, June 24, 2020

B. 1956 in Geelong, outside
of Melbourne, Australia;
Lives and practices in
Melbourne, Australia

Inventing New Ways of Making
Ruptures and Extrusions
The Raw and the Cooked
Learning from Others
Scalelessness

Architects are typically interested in diversity, insisting that every project is different, but as a critic, I want to establish what makes your work special and find patterns that repeat. How do you see the common thread in your work?

You are right, and I am more aware of the variants, not the parallels of my projects. Our buildings are creatively opportunistic, and we are strongly engaged in the process of making them. I think what's common is a sense of care and intent for the human experience. Much of our work is about the assembly of fine details, of which I am always very critical. Forms and silhouettes are important, but when you come closer it is all about details, which translate into how the building is experienced at the individual level.

One notion I am particularly interested in is "scalelessness." It gives us freedom. It broadens possibilities. A vase may give shape to a room, a house, or a large urban complex on the scale of a city. Ideas can migrate from scale to scale. That's why we undertake residential projects. I enjoy the interaction, the intimacy. There is a greater level of detail and refinement. They allow a personal level of engagement with the client where great rewards can be found. I like the scale and character of enclosure that residential projects provide. And working on some of the smallest details provides us with a range of possibilities. And, sometimes, details worked out in our houses are translated into some of our larger projects. Of course, they are not simply about scaling things up, but what these small buildings teach us is that even very large buildings must incorporate important qualities such as intimacy. And following the same logic, some civic qualities of large buildings can be drawn into family homes. This translation from small to large and back is both vital and fascinating.

Portrait: John Wardle (photo © Pier Carthew) **Top:** John Wardle Architects, Shearers Quarters, Bruny Island, Tasmania, Australia, 2008–11 (photo © Trevor Mein) **Bottom left:** John Wardle Architects with NADAAA, Melbourne School of Design, Melbourne, Australia, 2009–14 (photo © Peter Bennetts) **Bottom right:** John Wardle Architects, Captain Kellys Cottage, North Bruny Island, Tasmania, Australia, 2015–16 (photo © Trevor Mein)

Portrait: James Wines (photo © Andreas Sterzing) **Top:** SITE, *Best Products Forest Building*, Richmond, Virginia, 1979 (photo courtesy SITE) **Bottom left:** SITE, *Highrise of Homes*, 1981, project (drawing by James Wines, courtesy SITE) **Bottom right:** SITE, *Antilia* "Vertiscape" Tower proposal, Cumbala Hill, Mumbai, India, 2003–04, project (watercolor by James Wines, courtesy SITE)

"The Point Is to Attack Architecture!"

In a way, you use every one of your projects as an opportunity to offer a particular critique of the built environment and public space. How do you see your role?

All my work has something to do with a critique of architecture, its context, and its means of construction. It is about inversion, fusion, intervention, exaggeration, or taking apart and examining various elements to suggest an alternative point of view. The process has always been more interesting to me than a finished building. The point is to attack architecture! [Laughs.]

The whole profession is often too pretentious, humorless, and conservative. Early on I had begun to feel that a sculpture sitting on a pedestal was irrelevant. The more inclusive the art, the more interesting it gets. For example, the main idea motivating the early Best projects was to put art where you least expect to find it—especially in the junk world of commercial strips—and then use unfamiliar (and sometimes humorous) elements as a criticism of architecture itself. The Richmond Best store offered an ideal opportunity for the fusion of nature and architecture. The key to virtually all of SITE's work is a response to context. Or the Highrise of Homes celebrated personal identity in a typical cityscape, where anonymity and faceless habitat prevail.

We all know what is conventionally expected of architecture in terms of shelter, function, and design. So, I have spent a lot of my life asking, "What else could a building mean?" My intention was to encourage the public to re-think what they already assumed they knew about architecture. I think the point is, if you practice architecture without bringing ideas from other sources and disciplines, after a while your work becomes boring. The conventional skill of merely crafting good-looking formalist buildings wears very thin. You need to explore territories where you force yourself and the public to think differently. A continuously questioning discourse is the life's blood of art and culture. Architecture is not about what it is but what it makes you think about.

In conversation with James Wines of SITE, Architect

Artist's home in SoHo, Manhattan, New York, USA, November 17, 2015

B. 1932 in Oak Park, near Chicago, Illinois, USA; Lives and practices in New York, USA

Dematerializing
Interaction
Symbiosis
Inverting
Fusing

251

"The Only Way to Preserve Nature Is to Integrate It into Our Built Environment"

In conversation with
Wong Mun Summ and
Richard Hassell of WOHA,
Architects

Palazzo Bembo in Venice, Italy,
May 27, 2016

Wong Mun Summ: B. 1962 in
Singapore; Lives and practices
in Singapore

Richard Hassell: B. 1966 in Perth,
Australia; Lives and practices in
Singapore

Erasing Boundaries
Responsible
Delightful
Sensuous
Generous

One of your exhibitions was called Breathing Architecture.
*Is this the key principle of your work—to create buildings
that breathe?*

RH: Absolutely. That exhibit was held in Germany where
regulations require buildings to be entirely sealed from
nature and provide a very controlled environment. But
for us it was important to demonstrate the alternative of
porous and perforated buildings, because in the tropics
the difference between comfort and something that's very
uncomfortable is just a matter of air movement. Sealing a
building means consuming a great deal of energy to create
comfort. Our other inspirations come from traditional arts
and crafts such as textiles and weaving. That informs us
about how to design our façades and other form-defining
components. And, of course, we are inspired by landscapes.
We aim at building a garden city and erasing boundaries
between architecture and landscape. In the Anthropocene
epoch, the whole world is a managed landscape. The only
way to preserve nature is to integrate it into our built
environment.

WMS: For us, shaping and forming buildings is all about
finding the best ways for providing breezes and air
movement. Air should be constantly moving across spaces
within buildings. As far back as at our universities, we both
studied environmental design with a focus on passive,
energy-efficient buildings. Introducing landscaping and
greenery and creating social spaces within our buildings
became the backbone and key features of our work. And in
Singapore, we are forced to think about high density. In the
future, cities will be much more connected and truly three-
dimensional. In the past, the focus was on machine-looking
aesthetics, whereas now the goal is to make our cities
more livable. Our ideal is to create a comfortable garden
suburban experience and then replicate it vertically through
a megastructure for everyone to enjoy.

Portrait: Richard Hassell and Wong Mun Summ (photo © Studio Periphery) **Above:** WOHA, PARKROYAL on Pickering, Singapore, 2007 (photo © Patrick Bingham-Hall)

253

Vladimir Belogolovsky (b. 1970, Odessa, Ukraine) is an American curator and critic. He graduated from the Cooper Union School of Architecture in 1996. After practicing architecture for 12 years, he founded his New York–based Curatorial Project, a nonprofit, which focuses on curating and designing architectural exhibitions worldwide. Belogolovsky is an Academician of the International Academy of Architecture in Moscow (IAAM) and IAAM's official emissary in the United States. He writes for *Arquitectura Viva* (Madrid), *SPEECH* (Berlin), *AZURE* (Toronto), and is a columnist on *ArchDaily* and *STIR*. He has interviewed more than 400 leading international architects and has written 15 books, including *China Dialogues* (ORO Editions, 2021), *Iconic New York* (DOM, 2019), *Conversations with Peter Eisenman* (DOM, 2016), *Conversations with Architects* (DOM, 2015), *Harry Seidler: Lifework* (Rizzoli, 2014), and *Soviet Modernism: 1955-1985* (TATLIN, 2010). Belogolovsky has curated and produced over 50 international exhibitions. Among these are *Architects' Voices Series* (World Tour since 2016), world tours on the work of Emilio Ambasz, and Harry Seidler, an American tour on Colombian architecture, *Green House* exhibition at the *Zodchestvo* International Architecture Festival in Moscow (2009), and *Chess Game* exhibition for the Russian Pavilion at the 11th Venice Architecture Biennale. He has lectured at universities and museums in more than 30 countries. In 2018, Belogolovsky spent the fall semester teaching at Tsinghua University in Beijing as a visiting scholar.

Portrait: Vladimir Belogolovsky inside Refik Anadol's installation *Machine Hallucination*, New York, USA, 2019 (photo © Alina Nemirovskaya)

Published in Australia in 2022 by
The Images Publishing Group Pty Ltd
ABN 89 059 734 431

Offices

Melbourne
6 Bastow Place
Mulgrave, Victoria 3170
Australia
Tel: +61 3 9561 5544

New York
6 West 18th Street 4B
New York City, NY 10011
United States
Tel: +1 212 645 1111

Shanghai
6F, Building C, 838 Guangji Road
Hongkou District, Shanghai 200434
China
Tel: +86 021 31260822

books@imagespublishing.com
www.imagespublishing.com

All photography is attributed in the Project text, unless otherwise noted. Cover: Adjaye Associates, The Webster, Los Angeles, USA, 2020 (photo © Laurian Ghinițoiu); page 2: Alberto Campo Baeza, Gaspar House, Cádiz, Spain, 1992 (photo © Isao Suzuki); pages 6 and 11: Ma Yansong and Olafur Eliasson: *Feelings are Facts*, installation, Ullens Center for Contemporary Art (UCCA), Beijing, China, 2010 (image courtesy MAD Architects)

Vladimir Belogolovsky extends his gratitude to Charles Linn, who assisted him with streamlining the texts.

A catalogue record for this book is available from the National Library of Australia

Title: Imagine Buildings Floating Like Clouds: Thoughts and Visions
            on Contemporary Architecture from 101 Key Creatives
Author: Vladimir Belogolovsky
ISBN: 9781864709087

This title was commissioned in IMAGES' Melbourne office and produced as follows:
Editorial Georgia (Gina) Tsarouhas, Jeanette Wall *Graphic design* Ryan Marshall
Art direction and production Nicole Boehringer

Printed on 140gsm Da Dong FSC® wood free paper, by Artron Art (Group) Co., Ltd, in China

IMAGES has included on its website a page for special notices in relation to this and its other publications. Please visit www.imagespublishing.com